THE STAGE IS YOURS

Exploit Your Potential

by

Sylvester Ryan Pontes

First published in 2020
Printed in India at: DGV Company

ISBN 978-93-89058-42-0

The Write Place
A Publishing Initiative by Crossword Bookstores Ltd.
Umang Tower, 2nd Floor, Mindspace, Off Link Road,
Malad West, Mumbai 400064, India.

Web: www.TheWritePlace.in
Facebook: TheWritePlace.in
Twitter: @WritePlacePub
Instagram: @WritePlacePub

Dedication

This book is a dedication to the many people in my life who have been instrumental in every part and aspect of me not only being a Master of Ceremonies or a Speaker but also becoming the person that I am today.

Aknowledgement

I'd like to start by saying that God is everything to me. All that I am and the success I have and will achieve I owe to God completely. Thank you, Jesus, my Lord, for blessing me with talents that I am able to put to use to and touch people's lives. His grace has helped me to achieve things beyond my reach and capacity. I never ever thought I would write a book. But I'm grateful to the Almighty for guiding me and using me as an instrument to make a difference in people's lives. Without Him I am nothing; with Him I can achieve everything. The very fact that I am breathing to live through the success I have achieved in my life is all because of His blessings. All the credit is deserved by God alone. His love and grace upon me has bought me this far and I believe will take me to places that He wants me to see. This book is also my testimony of how faith in God and hard work can take you to heights. I pray you get to know His love like I did.

My beautiful and loving wife Rochelle Rodrigues who has always been the backbone of my life. She supported me through the toughest juncture of my life and is the reason why I dare to dream big and pursue things beyond my potential. She has been my encouragement to not give up and just keep moving forward. Thank you for being with me in the bad times, especially when I had the world against me, when I was completely broke. You still stood beside me as a rock. The great times for us have just begun and we have a long way to go.

Family: I'd like to thank my parents for the gift of life. My aunt Maria Pontes who gave me an opportunity to rebuild my life and ensured all my actions and energies were diverted towards building a goal and being a better human. A big thank you to the Rodferntes family for accepting me as your own. Each one of you is dear to me.

Ami Seth — Thank you for instilling within me the confidence of truly believing my calling in life. You planted a seed within me that I'm sure I didn't let go to waste. Today, I believe that I can achieve whatever I want and that every dream and ambition in life is possible. Without you I wouldn't be anywhere close to where I am. Thank you is a very small word to express my gratitude for the impact you've made in my life. You are 'The Mentor' of my life. You were always a call away whenever I needed you. I remember a conversation between us a few years ago. I had asked you how I would pay you back what you've done for me. You humbly replied saying, "Whenever in the future, if you end up writing a book mention my name." This dedication is a very small gesture compared to the magnitude of change you have brought in me.

Friends are people you choose to have in your life. I believe that *our company decides our destiny*. I have been blessed to come across the right people in my life. Life is all about relationships that you build and I cherish each one of them. I'd like to make a special mention here for a few:

Sanatan Bhaskar — For always being there as a friend and as an elder brother whenever I needed you. Thank you for all your advice.

My Critics: While coming up with content for this book, I needed inputs from others on whether was I on the right track and was able to consistently deliver my message to my readers. I want to extend a special thank you to Anjana Iyer Castelino, Leesha Vachhani, and Foram Ajani, who were a blessing in disguise. They guided me with timely feedback and helped me highlight areas I missed out on and restructure my ideas in an organized manner. Thank you for spending valuable time reading my chapters time and again and helping me enhance them with your inputs. This wouldn't have been possible without you guys!

Kevin Menezes — Throughout the journey of writing this book, you have inspired me to just keep going in spite of me being completely dislodged with my content. Thanks for helping me streamline my thoughts and guiding me, not only with this book but also spiritually.

– **Sylvester Ryan Pontes**

My Pledge

I am an awesome creation of God,

Fearfully and wonderfully made in His likeness.

I have greatness bestowed within me.

I shall never doubt my talents, but use them to my full potential to glorify God.

I do not bow down to situations; instead, my will to never give up shall change situations in my favor.

I am strong and no matter what situation tries to knock me down, I shall rise again each time stronger than before.

You may see me struggling, but you will never see me quit.

I am put on this earth for a purpose. I will find my true calling in life by God. And will do it unto His will.

The things you love doing casually can
end up becoming your career.

– Sylvester Ryan Pontes

Forewords

His story is inspiring - **Clince Varghese - TEDx speaker, Indian TV host.**

Lucid, Straight to the heart Dialogue. - **Avirat Shete - Tedx speaker, Director of Shete's Institute of Academics Pvt limited.**

Two words that that have always stuck in my mind and had me intrigued from the very the first time I heard them are 'ikigai' and 'meraki'. Combining 'iki' – life and 'gai' – value, ikigai is about finding joy in life through purpose. Meraki, on the other hand, is doing something with soul, creativity or love; to put something of yourself in your work.

Smart, enthusiastic and straightforward - this book is all about finding your ikigai and meraki, an excellent primer for anyone aspiring for a career on the stage and a handy guide to navigate life and accomplish your dreams. - **Kannan Sivasubramanian - CEO at Aranca**

Sylvester is a sage on the stage and a guide on the side. This book is a must read for anyone who wants to do something with life. - **Dr. Jagat Shah, Founder - Mentor on Road & Smart village**

Introduction

The intention of writing a book never crossed my mind, although it was on my vision list. One day, I thought I've been reading so many books and all of them in some way or the other relate to experiences based on real stories. So I decided why not go ahead and share my own experiences, especially those related to my hobby-turned profession. In my opinion, it is one of the best careers I could have chosen.

This book will not only give you a glimpse into the life lessons I have learnt as a Master of Ceremonies but will also help you find what your calling in life is. It will guide you through thoughts to identify your talents, and how they can be used to encourage and challenge yourself to follow your inner instincts and help you find what describes the real you. I must be honest in telling you this: I started writing this book with the intention of restricting it to compering and public speaking only, as both professions are interlinked and require similar skills. But after deep consideration I realized how challenging it was for me to decide to take up my talent as a career. While wrestling with these ideas I even found out that people usually hesitate to pursue their hobbies/talents as careers for many reasons. I wanted this book to be the breakthrough that could give people belief and courage to push forward, to believe in themselves to make the move and conquer what they believe in.

In this book, I've tried to cover most points to give you an insight into how to overcome this hurdle, as even I struggled through it before achieving victory. I hope my success story helps you to live your vision. I am certain it will ignite a spark in your minds to reach for your dreams. It will teach you how not to give up but be resilient and persistent to fight for the life you want to live. It will show you that your dreams (whatever they may be) are not far beyond your reach. It's possible to live a life on your own terms and conditions. And if you're not there yet, this book will show you how to get there.

The Stage Is Yours is a call to each and every one to take charge of your life. It will help you identify who you are as a person, it will give you ideas about how you can develop your talents and how small steps each day will help you feed your dream. This book is written with the intention to inspire every age group to follow their inner voice and bring creativity to every aspect of your work and personal life. No matter what stage of life you are at, you're just one decision away from making it big. This may not be the best written book, but it will surely guide you into deep thought and cause you to wrestle with your conscience so that you make an impact in your life and burst out of obscurity to get all that you want and deserve in life.

If you only nurture the gifts and talents that God has bestowed within you, nothing can stop you from flying high.

Contents

Contents

Discover Your Gift

Your gift will make room for you.
Proverbs 18:16

Chapter 1

What Is A Gift?

What is a gift? A question like this could have a very simple answer; yet, we wrestle with finding one. How does one figure out what is one's gift? The gift of life is the most valuable gift given to us by God but it becomes an incredible gift when you discover the 'why' part for your life.

Take a look around and see how many people you know have it figured out. You'll be surprised by the fact. How many of them have found the 'why' in their lives? Often, you face an emptiness within you and this thought runs in your mind — there has to be something more to this life. That's because there is certainly more in life that is unknown to you.

The 'why' part came to me when I discovered something that God gave all of us. He has blessed each one of us with a unique gift. Never is a soul created without a gift and sent to earth. It clearly means that each one of you is gifted. And each one has a different gift. Some can sing, others dance, one can bake better than others, some have a better hand at cooking, one can be a problem solver, some are good at talking, negotiating and sales, one could be good at humour and others are blessed with skills at argument and can take up the profession of being a lawyer.

Everyone has a gift. The only way to grow it is to attach yourself to your gift. I'm sure you are wondering how does one find out what his or her gift is?

According to Steve Harvey, "the thing you do absolutely best with the least amount of effort is your gift." When you decide to pursue your gift you don't struggle at what you do.

Where we go wrong is when we see what others do and begin to think that taking up their gift/job is the attractive thing to do. That's when you decide to leave your gift and start following a passion. At one time in my life I was passionate about being a pilot. But when I learnt what it entailed to become one, the thought flew out of my mind as a fast an airplane could, because I realized I wasn't meant for it.

Similarly, I had to find out what my gift was and when I really went back to my life I found out I could connect with people, convince and influence them. I never feared crowds or speaking on a stage. I was funny and would love to make people laugh by being humorous. Slowly, as I started pursuing my gift, it led me to what I wanted to become.

The book of **Proverbs 18:16 says**, '*Your gift will make room for you and bring you before great men*'. When you follow your God-given gifts, doors of opportunities start to open. The book of Romans 12:6 says, "*Having then gifts differing according to the grace that is given to us, let* *us use them.*" It encourages you to follow your gift, not passion. I have not made a penny with my passion. But my gift has blessed me with all I have now.

Take time and ask God what is your gift. Spend time with Him and He will reveal to you the secret that will lead you to your greatness.

All that you desire is possible to
achieve, only if you make it happen
and never quit
                    - Sylvester Ryan Pontes

Chapter 2

Your Gift Will Add To Your Wealth

I was always fascinated with being wealthy, reading about how to get there and how to make things happen. I would read success stories of industrialists, engineers, etc., and always would land at a sad conclusion: that it was not in my destiny to become wealthy. I would be demotivated at times, knowing that I was not as qualified as others to be at their level. And this thought would always fog my mind, including the middle-class upbringing by my parents — "Don't dream big, be happy with just enough. This is our life and we can't do anything more about it." I'm sure you must have heard some version of this from your parents at some point when you were a kid. According to them, they were right. But somewhere in my heart I knew I couldn't settle for this.

I believe each one of us has the right to wealth. And it does not matter where you come from or what you family background is. What makes you different from others is you yourself. Robert Mugabe says, "If you don't come from a rich family. A rich family must come from you." Travel the globe and you will never find another you. You are blessed with something unique, a gift, a seed within you. All you need to do is germinate that and it will lead you to your greatness.

Have you ever noticed this, trees that bear fruit — mango, banana, or apple — never consume their own fruits. Their fruits are consumed by us by paying for them. Have you ever seen a mango tree consuming its own fruit as food? I'm sure not. The reason I'm saying this is because the gifts you possess are the things that the world is looking out for. They need to be shared with others and are not for self-consumption. Let me explain it in this way, as a master of ceremonies and a speaker I get invited to perform and speak maybe for two hours and get a handsome reward for the same. People will reach out to you for the fruits that you possess and will pay you the price you demand for them. This is because what you possess means something to the rest as they don't possess it. I challenge you take me for my word. Your gift has the power to make people who don't like you come up to you and pay you for your services. People will make themselves available according to your time. I've seen this happen to me. So I tell you this from experience.

From the time I realized what I was good at, I strictly followed only those things and I have never looked back on that decision. I must say it's one of the best decisions of my life. Today, I have performed and hosted shows for people from all walks of life at locations that I never dreamed of. You will not find work hard when you're following your gift. It will become a source pouring into your wealth. Let me end by saying, "All that you desire is possible to achieve, only if you make it happen and never quit."

Identify Yourself

Knowing yourself is the beginning of
all wisdom."

– Aristotle

Chapter 3

My Journey

Well, this is my story and here it goes. I was born in Dubai as my parents worked and lived there. As a kid I was well kept and the apple of my parent's eyes. I owe it to my mom for instilling in me the habit of always participating in school events like singing, poetry competitions, and skits. So the fear of being on stage was killed right from the start. Since the age of four, I had been on performing on stage but I never knew that this would one day be a career. I would call myself an above average student at academics, but when it came to extra-curricular activities I was great.

As I grew older we moved to India, and once I reached the age of 16, I started singing in bands at both college and intercollegiate festivals and bagging prizes. I thought of taking up singing as a career, but stumbled upon the concept of being an Anchor or Master of Ceremonies. I would watch others hosting shows in colleges, at weddings, and on television. Then started the wait to be invited at weddings just to watch the master of ceremonies. It would give me a different kind of pleasure to see them perform, their dialogues, and humor. Deep down in my heart I wanted to learn more about this profession.

When the invites stopped coming, I must admit, I started gate-crashing weddings during my teens at my church hall.

At least 30, I would say (please note, 30 is a modest figure I have given here so that you don't judge me). For me it wasn't about the lavish food but instead to watch the emcee. I won't lie, I had mastered the art of gate-crashing at weddings and was a pro at it. After learning and making mental notes of the flow of the event, I thought I knew it all. And I wanted to host weddings. But my age was a barrier for me. Who would hire a young, skinny chap at 19 who looked like a pack of bones? No couple would want the hassle of trusting someone young with their big day.

I tried pitching to family, friends, my office colleagues, church etc. Most of them said, "You're too young, you're not tall enough to be an emcee, you won't be seen in the crowd, who will hire a skeleton, you're not funny, no one hires a kid." All these were the encouragement I received from those I thought I knew very well. I was shattered and thought to myself that these guys know me and maybe they are right.

Though demotivated I couldn't stop thinking about the stage, and picturing myself on it. They almost killed my dream. But as Les Brown says, "Don't let anyone's opinion about you end up becoming your destiny." I was strong in spirit, that I was going to capture the stage. I was not going to stop what I believed in. I didn't mind if I failed, but I wanted to have a go at it, come what may.

It is better to be prepared for an opportunity and not have one, than to have an opportunity and not be prepared.

- Les Brown

Chapter 4

Be Prepared

There was a storm in me that ate up my peace each time I would ponder about my worth, and what I should take up in terms of a career. I was fascinated with what others did and was planning to pursue those things. As I mentioned in the previous chapter, it took me time to figure out what I was good at. When I tracked back along memory lane I remembered singing on stage, acting, being funny, and never fearing being on stage. I would always seek an opportunity to work in those fields but didn't know how.

I would spend time looking at singers or master of ceremonies and make notes of how they behave and keep a close eye on their body language, etc. Through all these times I waited patiently for my time, and for an opportunity. This waiting period was killing me inside. I was like a volcano from within, hungry for that opportunity. If anyone gave me the microphone I would rock their world. I had heard this from Les Brown, "It is better to be prepared for an opportunity and not have one, than to have an opportunity and not be prepared." These were the only words that kept me going at that time.

After waiting for a while I came across the opportunity I always wanted. And it arrived when I least expected it.

When it arrived I knew deep inside, it was my moment to rise and shine.

I'm sure you would love to know more about it. And I tell you it was a hell of a ride. To know more turn to the next chapter…

Sometimes opportunity will knock
when you least expect it, all you need
to do is act on it.
- Sylvester Ryan Pontes

My First Break

I have always had the pleasure to tell people how I landed into this profession. I did have the skills, but never thought I would stumble on it when I least expected it. I won't keep you waiting for long. Here's how the story goes.

I was a very fun-loving powerhouse of energy as a kid and youth among my friends. I began working at an early age, and my first job was at a call center in Mumbai. A colleague of mine was getting married and I was assisting her with the wedding preps. Since her fiancé was also in the same office, they knew me very well and asked me to be the Best Man for the wedding, which I gladly accepted. Oh! What a feeling it was to be a best man. I must admit I have thoroughly enjoyed being best man for many other weddings too. You get a new suit and a beautiful bridesmaid (that you may want to potentially date), new shoes and most importantly a lot of attention as well. But at this wedding my desires were short-lived.

The night before the wedding, my friend received a call that her emcee wouldn't be able to make it for the wedding the next day. Tension, shock, and worry was all over the room as we tried to connect with people to find an emcee. Through all this chaos, at the back of my mind I was waiting for that opportunity, lurking around like a hungry vulture for its prey. That's when my friend decided that I would be the master of ceremonies for the evening, as I knew the families and they knew my level of craziness. I was happy at that moment, but thinking about the pressure it felt like I was hit by a cannonball. My head started spinning as I had never ever done a wedding. And that was how I was fired as best man and hired as master of ceremonies. The good part here was I was allowed to keep the suit.

Although I was nervous, I knew this was my time to rise. And that I couldn't let nervousness steal the moment that I had been waiting for. Sometimes, opportunity will knock when you least expect it, all you need to do it act on it. That is what I did. Now, with less time at hand and a lot of work to do, I needed to brush upon what I had been preparing all this while. With the help of the internet of course, the speed of which my turtle could also beat in the year 2009. At that hour of the night YouTube came to my rescue as I searched online for jokes and the duties and nuances of an emcee.

The next evening from what I can recollect, I made a few mistakes which I covered up quickly as the crowd did not know what I had prepared. But overall the energy and my humor won the hearts of the people. I did mention that time to the crowd that this was my debut. But the turning point came when I received a standing ovation from the guests and two more enquiries to host weddings. And that's how I arrived in this profession of spreading smiles, making memories, and building new relationships.

From the age of 19 to date, this has been one of the best careers I have been in and it's a blessing from God that I have been able to continue for a decade now. I have never regretted it one bit. This profession has taken me to places and heights that I may have never reached as an individual.

This book is a deep dive into my journey, my experiences, business ethics, morals, and my trade secrets, and how I made it all happen. If I could achieve what I desired, so can you. If you are already there, it will show you how to move to the next level and boost your performance. It will help you manage sticky situations where in only your presence of mind can get you out.

I hope this book helps you to the fullest at being what you want to be and achieving your goals.

Life is too short and we spend so much time in things that lead us nowhere rather than doing the things that really matter.

- Sylvester Ryan Pontes

Chapter 6

Identify The Agents Hampering Your Dreams

What's hampering your dreams? This is the easiest thing to identify within ourselves, but we often fail to acknowledge it. There may be times when other individuals may even mention it to us, but we hesitate to pursue it further. Nevertheless, this is the easiest thing to identify within ourselves. It could be fear, lack of confidence, pressure of trying the unknown, or some other reason.

I can tell you this because at one point in my life I was clearly living a life I didn't want to live. So I can absolutely connect with you on this feeling of being frustrated within. After leaving my sales job when I was young, I wanted a hike in my pay and started working in a customer service profile. The pay was good but the job was so boring and I couldn't understand anything they would train us on. The first month went by somehow, and I thought to myself, let me continue with it as the money was better. But somehow I wasn't able to relate to the job. Come Monday, I wasn't even motivated to get out of bed and go to work. This was my first wake-up call.

I started noticing that I would feel suffocated and not excited from within at work. I remembered the days I would work at sales and the joy I would receive in closing deals.

Not forgetting the incentives I made as well. I realized that I was not going to be able to survive in this profile for long. And eventually, in three months, I quit my job. I then found another job in sales that revived my excitement. It was the same feeling I got when I first picked up the microphone to host a show. And it's been 13 years approximately I've been into sales and 10 years as an emcee.

I can relate with people when they can't get out of bed in the morning. When you struggle to step foot in the office premises. When you're at Monday but dreaming about the next weekend already. When Monday is a burden, Tuesday and Wednesday is a cross you can't escape, Thursdays get you excited, let one more day pass till Friday comes. Even God worked six days and rested on the seventh day after creating so much. And we people sometimes haven't created anything in five days and yet we strive to reach the weekend. If you come back from a holiday but you're already planning another one, this is something you need to consider seriously.

What I'm about to mention now is something I came across while watching a video of Les Brown that caught my attention. He said 48 percent people get a heart attack around the world on Monday between eight am and nine am. This is while they are heading to work or should I mention a place that they don't like spending time at. I don't mean to scare you but the truth is we aren't living what we are on earth for. We live life as though we are in a race, where in the end you just stop living. Let me tell you there is a way out of that.

I have friends who were frustrated engineers and bankers, that's what I called them. One of them loved food and the other one loved to sing. And after a lot of thought both quit their jobs. Now, one is a food taster for a company in India that rates food and is also a blogger. The other friend met up with a few musicians and set up a band. Slowly and steadily both of them picked up the pace of what they loved doing and now, each day, they live life to the fullest enjoying what they do. Life is too short and we spent so much time in things that lead us nowhere rather than doing the things that matter.

Don't compete with the world, beat
your own milestones.
- Sylvester Ryan Pontes

Chapter 7

Find Your Seed

I believe God has placed us on earth not empty-handed, but with talents, which I call *seeds*. He has gifted us these talents so that we can make complete use of them, be fruitful, and glorify His name. But sometimes it seems completely impossible for us to figure out what our talent or seed actually is. Let me start by saying if you focus on your education, your reach is limited. On the other hand when you focus on your talent, it will take you places you might have never ever imagined.

Talent combined with the fuel of education can prove to be immensely fruitful. The only challenge is to identify what our seed is. The day you realize and find what it is, it will be your rebirth. If you nurture that seed, come what may, no man on earth will be able to stop you from reaching your destiny and living up to your full potential. But the most important part is to identify what your seed is and for that you must have a vigilant eye. If you are a parent, it starts with recognizing your kids from an early age. Notice them very closely as you never know what they stumble upon could be something that could change their whole life and end up becoming a career.

Nowadays, very few parents encourage their children to pursue their hobbies. I encourage everyone to pay close attention to their gifts — because it's only your gifts that will take you to destinations you may have never dreamed of. When you fail to identify the talents you are blessed with, it is only because you haven't spent time getting to know yourself. That is purely because you are distracted by the noise around you. Which leads you to being asleep and at the same time being a slave in terms of doing a job that is not truly meant for you. This way you're not only frustrating yourself, but also your company. Most people waste too much time trying to imitate somebody else's talent rather than focusing on their own. We spend so much time imitating others. This is why we get distracted from so many revelations about our own self. The biggest mistake one can make is completely ignoring his or her talent. I understand that we are brought up thinking that getting a good education and finding a good job are the sole purposes of our existence. I agree this was the situation earlier, but if you look at today's scenario things have changed drastically. Today, if you graduate from an expensive institution you get two things: a degree and a BIG FAT BILL to go along with it. And then you end up working at odd jobs just to repay the loan taken out for education.

Don't get me wrong — I am not against education. What I am trying to say is that education is a must, but at the same time if you can focus on your talents, you will have a chance of reaping a better reward. I am not saying give your hundred percent towards nurturing your talent. Even a little effort daily can actually be more than enough. It is said that if you need to reach somewhere and you can't get there at once, do it inch by inch and eventually you will complete the yard.

I'm glad I was able to find what my seed was early in life. If you push yourself beyond your limit, the outcome will always be remarkable. Don't compete with the world, leave the world aside. Try beating your own milestones. And when you look back after all the effort you put in, your story will be enough to speak about your success.

Don't take your gift to your grave.
- Sylvester Ryan Pontes

Chapter 8

Use Your Gift

I have mentioned in the previous chapters that each one of us is gifted by God. It is up to us how we find out and invest in what we are blessed with. It may seem at times very difficult and tiring, but if you don't invest in yourself then who will?

A gift or talent if not utilized remains like a dead seed. When you have been gifted by the Almighty, it is necessary to utilize your talents. Do not try to copy or imitate someone else's skill or talent. Remember you are at your best when you are authentic to your core. In simple words, keep it real and original. You and only you can suit you the best because as the Bible says *you are fearfully and wonderfully made in his presence* (Psalms 139:14). If you spend some time with yourself in silence, your heart will help you figure stuff out. Most people do not find time for themselves and let distractions take over that silence. Consequently, their lives are lost in the noise.

At first, it may just be a skill or hobby but how you develop it really takes time, practice, and dedication. It's a continuous process and you need to train yourself each and every day to make sure you master the art of it.

I remember when I was a kid I would play cricket every day and would be great at fielding and batting. No matter how high the ball would go, I could easily catch it because I would play the game every single day. If you try to throw a ball at me today and ask me to catch it like I did in the earlier years I bet I wouldn't be able to do it. That's because it's been than almost 10 years since I've played the game. I can tell you that today I would totally suck at it. If you don't practice your gift daily, if you don't sharpen it, you will slowly start losing the art of using it. In short, if you don't use it, you lose it.

Sometimes, you may try things that would be completely similar to what others must have tried earlier and always reached a dead end. You never know reaching the dead end could also be a good place to start from. Never be afraid to think out of the box. It takes courage to move against the odds. And only the ones who dare to make the move and live the life they want, get what they want from life. There are those who keep cursing their destiny and blame the situation for not being able to move forward. The go-getters, on the other hand, always seem to find a way that will lead them where they ought to go. Decide for yourself which path you would like to take.

Obsession can make your
dream a reality.
                    - Sylvester Ryan Pontes

Chapter 9

Be Obsessed

Most people may misconstrue being 'obsessed' as being motivated, but obviously these are two different words and mean two different things. Motivation won't keep you up all night, obsession will. Motivation can only let a person do what he wants to do till a certain point and then it could stop. When you are obsessed it will lead you to do anything in the world to achieve what you want. When you're obsessed it really doesn't matter what stands before you. You will have the determination to walk up front and snatch what you believe is rightfully yours.

Obsession is when you are out of ammo and you still run out to the guy and take him out. Motivation usually does not make successful people — successful people are obsessed with their dreams and that takes them to the top because they are not afraid of failing and not afraid of taking risks. They face challenges with a smile and have an attitude that helps them to learn from their mistakes.

Let me present an example of motivation and obsession to you. It will give you a clear understanding and help you distinguish between the two. Every year on December 31, many people make a New Year's resolution to lose weight, take care of their health, and get back into shape. Till the first, second, third or maybe at the max the fourth week, these guys are usually in the gym cranking and banging gym equipment to the extent that other gym inmates start thinking this guy is a disciplined body builder. This activity continues and then there is a sudden change in the pattern. The person who would regularly spend three hours a day and seven days a week suddenly starts visiting the gym three hours and week and gradually to three hours a month. And then their resolution is postponed until the next new year. You must have noticed this happening to everyone, including yourself. There comes a time when you lose interest in a task that you had planned to undertake.

The only reason for this is because you were *motivated* to do it. Motivation is a state of mind, and when your focus shifts it diminishes your motivation. Obsession, on the other hand, ends up being your way of life. If you notice athletes or wrestlers, they are constantly in the gym right from three am to the time they are done. They portray obsession and are determined in their minds, that come what may they will achieve what they want to at any cost, at any price, and in any condition. When you are obsessed, your goals will be almost maniacal, and people who cannot adjust to your work ethic or thinking will start giving you titles like 'workaholic', 'impossible thinking', 'huge goal setter', 'irrational talker', etc. But don't be disappointed because these people are those who do not think big and have no regards for their own goals. When people who have no goals and find your goals are huge and humongous, they often criticize you. Understand this: you will even be criticized by own family members. Even Jesus was criticized by the people of his own hometown. Your obsession for your goals will make you a wolf, a cerebral assassin. But once you achieve your goal, you will realize that it was all worth the effort.

As I end this chapter I would like to remind you that obsession always needs fuel. You need to fuel your obsession daily without quitting at it. If at all you give up on your obsession, it indirectly means you gave up on your life. So stay obsessed. Be a hunter to achieve all that you want in your life. Obsession is a bit like 'madness' in a good way. It helps you get the best for you out of your life in this world. So, I say it again: be obsessed and stay hungry.

Pay the price today so that you
can pay any price tomorrow.
                              - Grant Cardone

Chapter 10

Are You Willing To Pay The Price?

Every successful person who has made it to the top has always toiled during his early days to make it where he is at his present. Every individual at the top I have studied or read their books have always had their share of the grind. Without paying the price with your time, energy, commitment, dedication, and sometimes even staying away from your loved ones, you can't get to where you want to be. It's the sacrifice you are willing to make to achieve what is dearest to you and what you need in life. It's always good to pay the price today so that you can pay any price in the future.

This is my cry to all the youth today who feel that it's good to enjoy the present and the future is left to those who live to see it. Change this perception, as time flies very fast. If you treat life easy when you are young, life will be hard when your old. And if you have a hard work ethic in your youth, the latter part of your days will be easy. Do not treat life casually, or you may end up a casualty.

It's good to take a break sometimes as we all need to celebrate our success, but let it not distract you from the larger goals you set in life. Sometimes, you just need to keep on going ahead even if the times are hard. And if you keep moving forward, the hard times will shape your character and integrity.

One example that comes to mind is cricket, a game that is played across the globe, and especially loved in India. I noticed that West Indians had a particular knack to bowl bouncers and trouble batsmen all around the world. Even the bowlers who weren't tall could efficiently bowl a beamer to make the batsmen go crazy. That's because West Indies, being an island country, is surrounded with beaches. Since there are very few places for kids to play, they all play on the sea shore. However, since the surface on the ground at the beach is not as hard as the one in the stadium, the bowlers have to add more muscle and energy to get the ball to bounce. After playing in such conditions over time, when the bowlers moved to a proper pitch meant for cricket. They would put a lot of muscle and energy in the bowling and the resulting beamers would not only trouble the batsmen, but get wickets too. That's how training through the rough times pays off.

It really doesn't matter how tough life may be, it is in such times that an individual carves his life and sketches his destiny. Your life is in your hands and life gives each one of us a paintbrush to paint our future. What you paint depends on you. You become what you think of yourself. So think and dream big and work towards it with the equal amount of passion so that you can live a life of abundance and teach others to do the same too.

Plan Your Journey

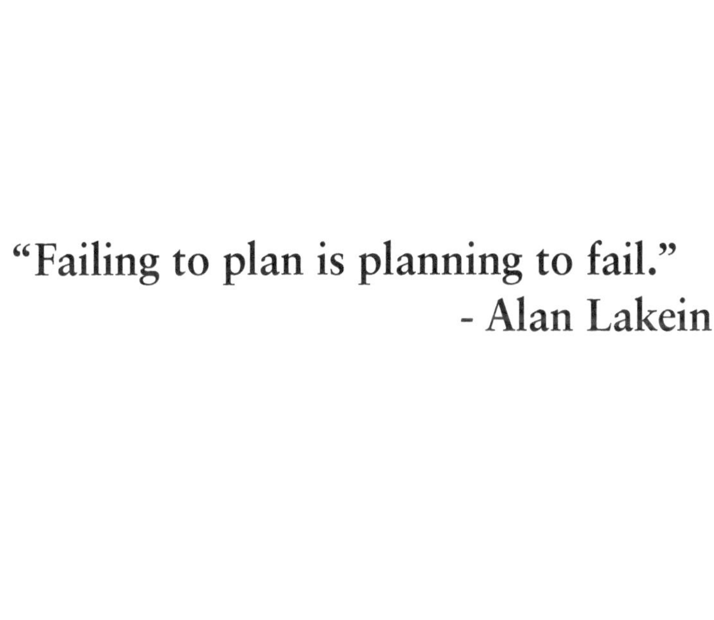

"Failing to plan is planning to fail."
- Alan Lakein

Chapter 11

Always Have A 'Plan A'

If you are aiming to take your life to a place where you've never reached before then you would need a plan to get there. In the same way most of us plan for where our life should lead. Apply the same attitude towards what you are aiming for and what you want to achieve. That's absolutely the right way to do things. And in doing so you also portray that you are a person of vision. Each one of us makes a plan on how to get there, and then just incase their plan does not work, they switch over to plan B to get to their desired vision.

I call this completely baseless, as if your vision is strong on plan A why have a plan B? That diverts you from from putting all your energy into achieving plan A. Your mind will tell you why worry when you already have a plan B. Gauge what is important to you in your vision, what you hold close to you and dream about making that your plan A and certainly not plan B. The world you know will tell you about keep another option in life, but if you look closely they are the same people who must have not gone far in achieving their dreams. Be a warrior for what you want in life. Never settle till you get there and the success to reach what you dream of will be absolutely sweet. Being on the top is a glorious moment. And when you look back at your path you will see it was worth the sweat and toil. Don't get caught up with the noise of the world, because every person has a different journey to take in life. Be focused on your life journey, that's it.

For those who are now wondering, in spite of all my effort in plan A if I fail, what then. The simple answer to it: Don't be afraid of failure. Treat failure as an event not a person. Failure is good if you learn from it. And if plan A comes crashing down go find another Plan A. And start putting your energy and soul into that. I'd like to share a story about a person I admire the most — Elon Musk, the owner of Tesla Motors. When he was to launch satellites into space everyone told him in his business not to do it as he had no expertise and if it failed he would be insolvent. Each satellite he launched would cost him 100 million dollars. He launched three satellites one after another at different intervals and all three crashed into the ocean. The people around him were furious and they didn't want him to launch the fourth satellite. If it would have crashed it would have been 400 million dollars down the drain. But that didn't stop Elon. He paid no heed to the negative stuff and learnt from his mistakes and failures, improved his launch plans, and when the moment came for the launch, it was nothing less than glorious. He launched it and it was successful. He believed in himself. He could have backed out but he stuck on to his Plan A and didn't go with Plan B.

So my advice to you, my friends, is simple. Don't let Plan B come in the way when you're at your A game. Be fearless and courageous along with having the belief that it's possible and you will make it. When your determination is strong and you never to give up, there is only one thing that will happen next — you will achieve.

You will never go broke from
investing in yourself.

- Anonymous

Chapter 12

Invest In Yourself

The biggest investment that one can make in his entire life is in himself. I strongly believe and practice this in my life, and it has helped me to move from where I was to where I want to be. It doesn't matter whether you are an emcee or in any other profession, if you do not invest in yourself you won't have the required fuel to reach beyond your potential. But if you have a fire in your belly and the desire to succeed you will fuel your purpose.

In the case of a master of ceremonies, when I mean invest in yourself, what I really mean is read books, try to identify new ideas that could add creativity to your event presentation. brainstorm and constantly keep yourself updated with new trends. Sometimes, detach yourself from the world and take a break. Breaking away from distractions will help you think clearly and figure things out. Learn from videos but don't steal someone else's ideas and present them as your own. You are equally gifted by God to use your own creativity. Reading will help you not only to excel but also to develop your personality. You will find that reading changes your way of looking at things and shapes your mind. When you have an ignited mind, ideas, success, wealth, and treasures are attracted to you.

Remember, whether you're in the profession of being an emcee or not, no one is going to come to help you make your dreams come true. *If you don't step up and take charge of your life now, someone else will drive your life and you will be left in the backseat with no control.* So, take action before it is too late.

Stop expecting your job to fund your vision. Your vision is probably bigger than your paycheck.

- Bishop TD Jakes

Chapter 13

Visualize Where You Want To Be

I'm writing this chapter to inform and alert you that the key to achieve your dreams is to visualize them as though you have already achieved them. Treat your life habits and train your mind as you want them to be. That way your mind is constantly progressing towards your desired goals.

Battles are won in the mind first and then executed in the world. Before I could become a master of ceremonies or speaker I would visualise myself speaking in front of a huge crowd. I wasn't there but I would imagine myself there already. I would practice my talks at home staring into the mirror. Every sentence I would speak, every intonation would be like how I would deliver it to a crowd of a thousand people. I would visualize that I was eye to eye with the crowd. This mind game continued till the day I got my first break. I was nervous, but when you have already won in your mind you will win on the battleground as well. When I walked out in front of the audience and spoke, it felt like I had been doing this all my life. There was no fear in my heart and that day I was a beast unleashed with no chains to hold me back. If I could describe it in one word I was *unstoppable.*

That's the reason why having a vision is necessary to achieve your mission. Set your sights on where you want to be and march forward with full force.

Then the Lord answered me and said:
Write the vision; make it plain on
tablets, so that a runner may read it.
For there is still a vision for the
appointed time; it speaks of the end,
and does not lie.
If it seems to tarry, wait for it;it
will surely come, it will not delay.
Habakkuk 2:2-3

Chapter 14

Make A Vision Board

In my early days I must admit that I wasn't a Bible reader, but after going through it on a regular basis I stumbled upon a chapter that I believed was for me. After reading it, it changed my life and my thoughts dramatically. I must add that the Bible is the greatest motivation book in the world and if you want to experience God speaking to you, read it.

What I read was from the Book of Habakkuk 2:2-3. *"Then the Lord answered me and said, Write the vision; make it plain on tablets, so that a runner may read it. For there is still a vision for the appointed time; it speaks of the end, and does not lie. If it seems to tarry, wait for it; it will surely come, it will not delay."*

As soon as I read it I grabbed a piece of paper to note down my goals and make a vision board. That night I remember I was on a rampage and continued to note down all the things I wanted in life.

Once I made my vision board, I put up copies in all the places I frequented — phone, bedroom door, work computer. The reason was now I knew what I wanted I didn't want to be distracted from those goals. My wife thought I was a lunatic but she had no choice; I was obsessed and unstoppable.

I had written down all that I wanted in my life, even goals that were big and seemed beyond my reach. I didn't want to be realistic and achieve small. I would rather aim for huge things and miss, than aim low and hit the mark. When you make your vision board I suggest that you go unlimited on your request list, as I believe God wants us to have everything but wants us to list them so that He can deliver them to us.

Please take this as personal advice from me as what I have mentioned above has really helped me. With total honesty in my heart I would like to share that I have come up from a life on the streets after I was asked to leave my home. So all that I am telling you are things I had to do from scratch and not things that were handed to me. I came across a Biblical scripture that said, *"You have not because you ask not."* This is a statement that shocked me. Most people don't have a life of their dreams, because they don't ask for it. If you don't ask for it, how will you receive it? Up your ask and He will increase His give.

The main reason people do not get what they want is because they don't make a vision board. I have studied many people who are wealthy and they wrote down their goals. I have visited a few successful people and after seeing their vision boards, I had to change mine. Every wealthy person knows this is the principle of success.

So take the effort to write down your visions. No matter how huge your ask is, don't feel shy because God is giving and will give you what you desire at the right time. Make sure you write everything in detail, write at least 200 things that you want, how many houses you want, how much money you want, the businesses you want to own.

It will be difficult, but do it. And once you wake up every morning go through that list. Let that be the first thing you do every day, before your mind gets busy. Go through the things that matter to you the most, let your mind feel it and know the direction it should work in.

Goals in writing are dreams with deadlines.

- Anonymous

Chapter 15

Write Down Your Goals

This has been the single most important secret sauce of my success and achievement. Though many shall differ from my thinking, writing down things you need in your life is instrumental in acquiring what you want from the Universe.

Why do I say it's the most important is because when you write down your goals and what you want it's a commitment you make to yourself. Your mind, which is the single most powerful entity in your body, reciprocates those ideas and programs you to work accordingly to want you want. It also cuts you off from the things that don't matter or add value.

You have to discipline yourself when it comes to your life. By writing your goals twice every day — as soon as you wake up and before you go to bed, a huge mental shift that takes place. Most of us make a New Year's resolution on the first day of the year and then after a week or two we forget what the plan was. When you write down your goals daily it keeps your mind alert about what you need to do to get where you want to be.

When you focus on and write down your goals 730 times year, the mind stays focused and the effort you put in will always bring a comparable output.

I was never a believer of what I have written here above till I wrote down my goals of owning multiple houses, writing a book, traveling and settling in a peaceful place. Although I have achieved most of my goals, I'm still to achieve a few more on my list.

When you write your goals, I advise you to multiply each item by 10. If you want to own 10 houses, write 'I already own 100 houses.' Do you think the effort it would take to own 100 houses would be the same as to own 10 houses? You know the answer yourself. It's always good to aim beyond your reach so you put in 10 times the effort to achieve them. And that leads to you acquiring results beyond your potential.

When you pen down your goals you breathe life into them. You give them an existence that before was only in thoughts. When you revisit them every day they end up chasing you till they are accomplished. It gives your life a direction and you start taking action accordingly. This may not be the case before you put your goals down I say have unrealistic goals so that you are constantly striving to accomplish them. Your goals should be so big that the issues of your life should look small in front of them.

Remember, most people live a life without goals and spend their life just fulfilling someone else's goals. Don't get lost with the crowd, sail against the tide. It's your life on the line. Take control of it now.

The trouble with not having a goal is
that you can spend your life running
up and down the field and never score.
- Bill Copeland

Chapter 16

Bring Life To Your Goals

If you've gone through the previous chapter on how to aim higher and set big goals. Let me inform you that having big goals is half the work done. That's just the first part. To achieve the goals one has to have the mindset and must take adequate action to make it happen.

It is not like making a resolution at the start of the year and then forgetting about before the first month ends. If you want to breathe life into your goals you have to meet them every single day. It is just like a relationship with your loved one. You need to visit your goal every day. When I say visit, I mean write your goals down daily, if possible, or glance through it at the start of your day and before you end your day. *It's better to know what you're going after and spend time on what you want. Wake up with an agenda.*

When you practice this on a daily basis it trains your mind. I usually write down my goals once when I wake up every morning and once before I go to bed at night. This is my daily activity and I do it without fail.

Let me tell you the science behind it. Our minds are very easily distracted as the day begins. When you write down your goals as soon as you wake up, before the noise of the world gets to you, you feed your mind with the things that you need. And that gives your mind the path it should lead you down for the day. At bedtime you revisit your goals by writing or reading them again. Feed your mind with the things you want to achieve. When you write down your goals it activates multiple senses of your body.

It is human nature to keep adding new goals to your list. And that's fine as long as you list it in writing. Even in ancient times, thoughts were recorded by writing. Similarly, if you write down the things you need you're breathing life into them and you will attract them.

Just for the sake of an argument I would like to seek your opinion. One person makes a resolution on the first day of the year and doesn't visit it for months together. Another person writes and reads his or her goals twice a day, 365 days a year. Who do you think will be able to make it to what they desire? You already know the answer. And I hope you are able to implement it and make it happen for your own success.

Just follow this for one year. Do this in faith, and read your list with the expectation that God will answer. I bet you, out of the 200 things you have written you will be surprised and happy to see that you will achieve at least 10 percent of your goals. I'm confident about this, because I have tried it and it did work for me. And I pray that it works for you too. I will be very happy to see each of you reaching your goals. Just believe and it will be done.

Don't compare your life to others,
there is no comparison between the
sun and the moon. They shine when it
is their time.

- Anonymous

Chapter 17

Stop Comparing

We live in a time when everyone desires to be famous. And in the age of social media, today we are in the race to portray an image to the world of a person we may not be in reality. Don't worry, even Jesus was asked by His disciples to prove to the people who He was. Every time there is unbelief in your heart, it will lead you to perform to prove something that you don't really believe. Have you ever noticed this? Speaking for myself, I have come across this a million times.

In such times you crumble under pressure to make sure you prove to others the point you want to make. And when you try to prove something to others, it takes away the joy from your heart. That particular task ends up just being an activity. Today, I'm scared for my kids; I grew up in an age where we always felt pressure, but in today's age we are witness to performance. Everyone performs for others, sometimes knowingly and sometimes not. For example, if you cook a good meal, its not complete unless you post an Instagram story about it. And this is dangerous, as we are not satisfied with ourselves the way we are.

Comparing your life to another person's life would only be right if you started at the same point. But in reality you will very rarely find such a case. Because no two people have the exact same life. Everyone in the world has a different story and purpose. Measure yourself from where you started and not from where others did. That is how you can identify the progress you have made. If you continue to compare yourself to others, you will miss out on what you're blessed with and start desiring someone else's blessings. This will lead you nowhere. It would be better to rejoice with what you've been blessed with, rather than eyeing someone else's gifts with disappointment.

The person who respects time is the
one that time respects.
                    - Sylvester Ryan Pontes

Chapter 18

Redeem Time

God gave every human on earth a common gift — TIME. A person living in any part of the world, whether he is rich or poor, has the same number of hours each day. The person you are and what you become depends on how wisely you use your time. As time cannot be stopped nor we can control it, every time a day passes by you lose time. A new year in your life is mainly to redefine your purpose, your life's purpose, to re-establish goals and move forward.

If you look at the other side, life is also the passing of time. Life on earth is stopped by time. As time separates your past from the present and future, it protects us from living in a particular situation. According to me it is the greatest commodity on earth given to human beings. We may not possess the same amount of money, but we have the same time. Hence, we use the term spend time. If you're broke that means you have spent time staying broke. It is so powerful that whatever you invest it in, you will become that.

Treat time as money. As you get older time diminishes. Time depreciates like money and can be devalued. Who you hang out with can help you depreciate your time or appreciate your time.

How you utilize your time as a youth will determine what you reap when you're old. It's an asset that once lost can't be regained.

Be picky about who you keep around you, personalities, words, and traits rub off naturally.

- Anonymous

Chapter 19

Choose Your Company

In the words of Les Brown, "If you run around with nine losers, pretty soon you'll be the tenth loser." That means the people you associate with decide where you reach in life. Choose the people you want to hang around with very carefully, because you are identified by the people you hang out with. If you associate with millionaires, there are high chances of you becoming rich.

The people that you invest your time with is the yield that you receive. Let me share a page out of my lifetime. There was a time I used to hang with my buddies from school and college. Some were the same age as me and some were older. Now when you're in your teens you end up experimenting with a lot of stuff, in the search of the unknown. At the age of 15, I smoked my first puff of cigarettes, started drinking alcohol, and gradually moved to drugs. I never knew that these things that looked 'cool' to me at the time, would be so life-threatening later. I knew it wasn't right what I was doing, but with my friends doing it seemed normal and classy. Once the news reached my parents, things got difficult. I was grounded at home, but I would still manage to do the wrong things. Somewhere down deep I knew the path I had taken was leading to self-destruction, but my friend circle was the biggest distraction, and I just couldn't move away from them. I felt like I was a part of a clique. It took me three years to realize what I had done to my life. I knew I had wasted time and health I could never get back. Moreover, my friends tried convincing me that there is no future in education. I figured out they had dropped out from college and had no plans to study further. I knew I had to get my life back on track, but was also afraid as I didn't want to lose them.

I must admit, it is hard but not impossible. I took a step in the right direction to turn the situation around. I started moving away from my friends and I started praying as well. While they noticed it, they would be vocal about it and try to pull me in on any occasion when we met. But each time that happened, no was my answer. I figured that some people would always want you to be at the same level as theirs or below. They wouldn't want you to move up the ladder. Now that's a cruel reality of the world and you just can't help it. They are afraid and insecure when you move higher than them and they are left behind. In short, crab mentality. They feel comfortable when you're at the lowest or with them.

The situation was getting difficult and suffocating for me. I had to make that move, it was high time to say goodbye to the group that was pushing me and my career into a grave. I started straying away from them and slowly the distractions disappeared and my addictions too. I could focus more on what I had to do. Infact, I could make time to meet more people with the same interests as me and ones who could show me my path and lead me. I would later be spotted with people who were goal-oriented and I learned a lot from them. And I made it a point to be around people who were more successful than I was. I would listen to their tips and advice. Although very young at that time,

I learnt how to dream and start visualizing what I wanted in life. It really helped me and made a difference as I could see the progress in my life.

For some it could be a difficult task to make a decision to move away from people who we are glued to. But the choice is yours; you've got to make a decision between your friends and your destiny. You friends will always be there, especially the ones who care. But never at the cost of you missing the train to your destiny. Everyone doesn't receive a second chance at that. So make wise decisions for yourself and your life. I'm sure what you choose will lead you to where you want to go. I remember my dad's words, "Show me your friends and I'll tell you the future your life is going to have." I took my time to realize it, but I now know what it really meant.

No temptation has overtaken you
that is not common to man. God is
faithful, and He will not let you be
tempted beyond your ability, but with
the temptation He will also provide the
way of escape, that you may be able to
endure it.

1 Corinthians 10:13

Chapter 20

Don't Lose Your Youth

One of my chapters in this book talked about redeeming time. Essentially, that speaks about managing time wisely and making the full use of every minute you have. We are all bound to follow a clock as our time on earth is also based on it. That is the only thing that is continuously ticking and we can not stop or control it.

Time is equally connected to your age, so do not lose the strongest part of your life — your youth. All the effort and struggle you put in making your life while you're young, you will benefit the fruits of it when you're old. Hence, it was said by Bishop TD Jakes, "If you don't devour something when you are young, you will have nothing to divide when you are old."

Most of today's generation take their grind very lightly, thinking that they will figure things out later in life. From the age of 20-35 years is the time when your body is at its best and is resilient enough to handle stress. This is the time when you put yourself to the test. You are also able to withstand multiple failures and try new things. If you invest this time in something fruitful, you will reap the benefits of it when you're older.

I'm scared for the youth today who say to me, "I can't make up my mind, I haven't figured it out yet, I wanted to try this thing but didn't like it." My advice to them is, "I think you better hurry." I've come across many people who idle the most productive time of their lives doing absolutely nothing. And when it's too late they try to make things work and expect wonders to happen. Once while I was streaming a video I came across a statement that caught my attention by Bishop TD Jakes, "There is an old person inside you that's depending on you to be smart. It's the person that you're going to be 30 or 40 years from now. Do not disappoint that person by being foolish throughout the strongest time of your life."

Let's be honest, you just cannot focus on your grind when your old, when your back is against the wall and your knees are weak. Because you can't function the same way you did when you were young and vibrant. Here is my advice for all my young readers. If you aren't among the ones putting their best effort to make something out of your lives now, don't even think you will be able to make it when you're older. It will be an ultimate disappointment. And I pray you don't walk that way.

If I turn back and look at my life, I'm glad I made mistakes. I'm not saying I was a saint, but I was guided onto the right path to do the right things and to be a better person. Or else if would have continued down the wrong path. I wouldn't have been able to even write this chapter today. It is difficult to avoid distractions when you're young, I say this from experience. The difficult path in life always leads to a pleasant end. So make the right choice because your life is not a joke, it's serious business. And time doesn't wait for anybody. So live well and lead a life that people reflect upon.

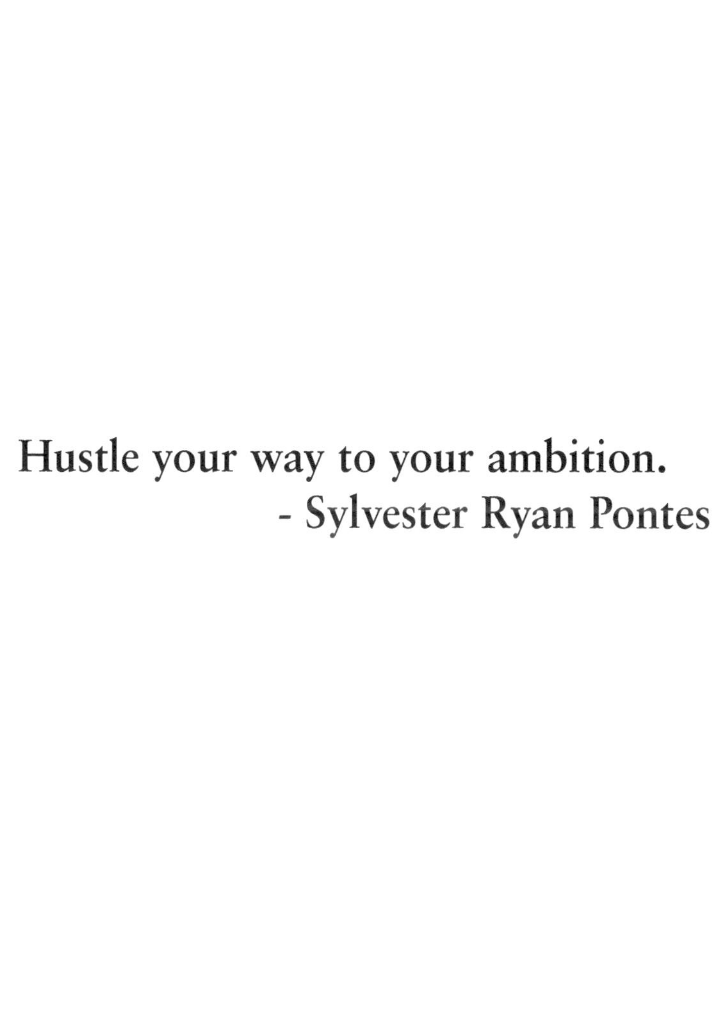

Hustle your way to your ambition.
                    - Sylvester Ryan Pontes

Chapter 21

The Hustle Is Never Easy

The path to where I am now has not been easy, especially because very few believed in what I believed within. And let me add, no success story is sweet without the hustle.

When you believe in what you want to do, you need to take equal action to reach there. After a few shows I had done, which was a glorious moment for me, there was a downfall in the enquiries. When this happened for the first few weeks it seemed normal, but gradually I figured out that no calls for shows meant people had forgotten me. I made calls to the people who I knew, but that was just a handful of contacts.

Create an identity in the market

I soon realized that if I played the small game I wouldn't be able to survive in this line. This is where my mentor helped me to plan a strategy that would give me a bigger break in the public domain so I could reach people who didn't know me. According to her, if people didn't know me they wouldn't do business with me. Which was absolutely true. In this age of social media I had no online presence, so we started with making a Facebook page and a YouTube channel. I started posting all my work on these platforms and also on Instagram and LinkedIn. I had made a goal that at least 5000 people would know me for my work at that time. Well I must say, it was a good place to start and I not only reached that mark, I exceeded it.

Network to increase your net worth

Well, YouTube, Facebook and other platforms will help people know what you do, but that's still not enough. You need to push and go the extra mile. I had to use all the rapport-building skills I had ever learnt. I would inform anyone and everyone that I was an emcee, giving them my business cards and receiving theirs. I started attending business seminars and talks where people from self-owned businesses attended, and forums like BNI. That's how I met new people with different influences and affluences. Getting to know them, speaking to them helped me get introduced into their circles. We would bump into each other at different events and that's how we reconnected and the relationship grew, thus leading them to recommend me to various people for events. That got me into corporates and I even connected with other master of ceremonies. That's how I grew my contacts. It wasn't easy at all, but the journey taught me how to play the game. That is what helped me to move forward. Networking has been one of the key factors of my business. What I have learnt from it is even when you're in need of business help others unconditionally. That way they remember your name and surely when the need arises, they will come back to you.

Rejection is part of the game

It you thought you were in for a rosy ride, let me clarify, there are going to be some bumps. The people you expect will do business with you will say no. Be prepared for rejection. Rejection has always served as fuel for me to accelerate. Take no offence to the person who may reject or not believe in your vision. There is a saying in sales, 'there are plenty of fish in the sea'. I have gone through so many rejections in the beginning of my career that now I don't fear rejection; it motivates me to reach beyond.

Keep pushing

If you plan to make any business, art or hobby a career, one has to add force and not settle. It takes time, commitment, and an never-giving-up attitude to reach the destination you desire. You cannot afford to lose focus till you reach there. I remember not when I was in my grind I would miss on my own family events to make sure I would make someone else's event memorable. The road is not easy when you have to miss family events. I had to hear a lot from my family and friends for not showing up at their events. But you've got to do what you've got to do. Some pleasures and time you have to sacrifice for a greater glory. You may lose some people along the way, but if they loved you they would understand. If they left you, you need to understand that they were never meant to be. Everyone can't walk the same path as you as everyone's priorities are different. Try overcoming the barriers with strong conviction and with the zeal to reach your destination, come what may. I'm telling you, looking at your determination, even the naysayers will give up crossing your path. I wish you all the hustle. Hustle your way to your ambition.

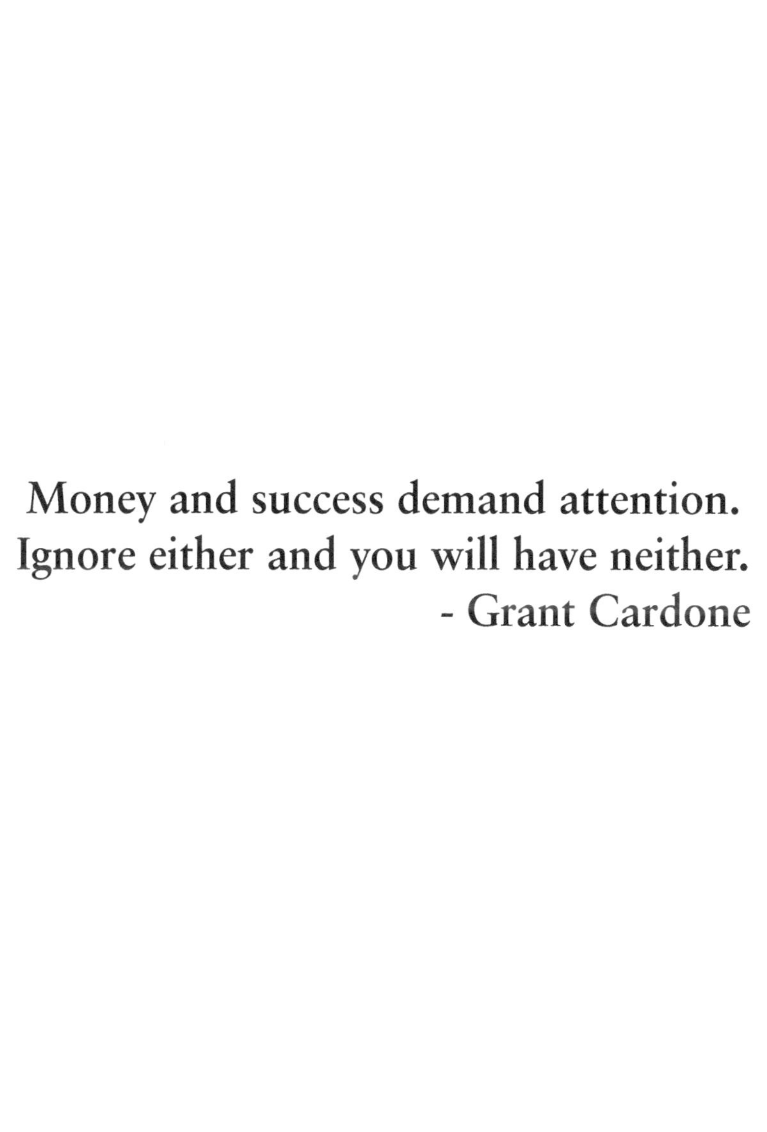

Money and success demand attention.
Ignore either and you will have neither.

\- Grant Cardone

Chapter 22

You Must Get Attention

After you have made a decision to take your gift into the market, unless people get to know you and what you're good at they won't be willing to do business with you. This is a process. It's very important to push yourself into the market. Social media is one of the things that can help you. But what really matters is how you get the people's attention. If you have to shout and make noise about it, do it. Whatever it takes to get yourself positioned in the market. Money follows attention. If you take your offerings to the street, people will come in contact with you and buy. You can't sell a thing sitting at home. It doesn't matter if you're loud or louder than anyone else in getting attention. I even suggest speaking to people you don't know. Business usually comes from strangers. You cannot stick to a certain circle or group. Branch out to expand your reach.

Critics

Remember, when you get enough attention you will also get criticism. And they will ask you to reduce your activity, because they cannot function according to your pace. Keep marching forward and don't get caught up in their words. Increase your action when this happens and make the critics burn out.

You need haters

When the attention you are getting becomes really loud, you will find haters. These are people who you will further market you and will be beneficial for you. You may find it strange, but I have personally thrived on hatred and that made me build my immunity against it. I love it when people talk about me, because they introduce me to a crowd that doesn't know me. People who love you will always spread the word across positively. I appreciate that, but their reach a limited. But understand this, if a hater speaks about you he will reach out to people who have nothing to do with you and yet will get to know about you. Some may not agree with me, but I'm convinced that it works. I've got the chance to work with clients who didn't know me, but heard some idiot using my name saying how arrogant I was. But when they connected with me the whole picture was different. Don't deliberately run in search of them. They will find you as you keep climbing the success ladder.

Admiration

Once you survive the last three stages I mentioned, you will be admired as you didn't give up, because you believed in yourself. Usually people don't take the first step and expect to leap directly to the last. The ones who usually burst out of obscurity, and do not confine themselves to petty comments from haters and continue on their journey are the ones who complete the whole cycle from where they started. These are the people who are glorified for their journey and success story.

911 for HELP!
Throughout this journey you're going to need a lot of help. And through this struggle the below chapters will help you cruise through your problems. I have always gone here for help and never came out empty-handed. You too will benefit from them.

When we keep God in first place,
everything else falls into place.
- Joyce Meyer

Chapter 23

Put God First

Everyone has a secret recipe to charge them, something that pushes them to do even better. It motivates them and helps them do whatever it takes to deliver an outcome beyond expectations.

My recipe is prayer. I may not be a very spiritual person, but I believe that moving a crowd of a thousand or two thousand is not an easy task, nor is it a joke. And I can't do it alone. This may not apply to everyone, as it is my personal belief. But I still believe I should share it as it has helped me. I must admit there are times I get goosebumps before an event. At such times my faith has stood by me. It has always been my strength, support, and my hope. What I am today is mainly because of my faith in God, Jesus Christ. Even before being a master of ceremonies and making up my mind about what to do in life, my faith helped me move mountains that couldn't be done by me alone. I cannot do anything without Him and I can do all things with Him by my side. I am what I am just because of Him and no one besides Him can take away His credit. Where I was, where I am, and where I want be is all known to Him. My belief in Jesus helps me do better than I can do by myself.

I remember my first event, how I was trembling in fear. I prayed before it started and till today before any event — be it a wedding, speaking engagement, or corporate event even if it's a small gathering — I pray. I ask God to give me the strength to entertain the crowd, to speak the right words, and help me do justice to the talents He has gifted me. I pray that He let me glorify His name as without those talents and gifts I cannot influence or connect with the crowd. I pray a short verse from the Bible that always motivates me: *"I can do all things through Christ who strengthens me."* (Philippians 4:13).

It has been 10 years since I began my profession of spreading smiles and creating memories, and I have never felt low. I have triumphed in situations with prayer alone. There are times when I'm not in 100 percent health, and yet just a simple prayer has worked wonders for me.

I pray and hope that this secret recipe of mine turns out to be the biggest winner and game changer in your life, no matter where you are and what you do in life. *No matter whatever you do in life, always put God first.*

If you're guided by God you will be
guarded by Him.
- Sylvester Ryan Pontes

Chapter 24

Have Faith — That's Enough

Have you ever noticed that we always strive to be and achieve our best? And in this effort we seem to put everything on the line to achieve our desires. There are many occasions when the desires of our heart overshadow the desires of God. Well, I'm sure this may have happened with you as well. It has happened to me on various occasions, that I have been blind to what God wants for my life. Sometimes when you are all fuelled up there comes a fall that brings a full stop to your dreams and life.

Take heart. What you feel is your downfall. Don't struggle against it. Sometimes accepting it is easier than challenging it. Worldly battles are fought with minds. But some battles are fought with faith. Let faith lead you to the right path. The good that you don't see will come to you at a time, which will be right according to His time. Don't let your short-sightedness rob you of the bigger picture that God has set you up for.

I added this chapter for a reason. As ambitious individuals, we look to the side that benefits us the most, not knowing that there could be times when things don't go as planned. Such situations leave us with a broken spirit. Let it be your faith that comes to your rescue, no matter how difficult it seems to get to the other end. The

Bible says if you have faith as small as a mustard seed you can command the mountain to drown itself in the sea and it will. And in desperate times when you can't stand the storms in your life, kneel and pray in faith and the storm will pass and clear skies will emerge. There will be times when your plans will be out of your reach even after prayer and penance. Don't lose hope. God's plans are greater than what your plans could ever be. There is a process to make a statue out of a rock. It takes countless hammer hits to make a masterpiece. The times of trouble in your life are not to punish you. God is using those hammer hits to make sure that your life is a masterpiece, a testimony to the world.

Before you throw in the towel, have faith because it is not over until you win. And when you walk in faith with the Lord, the Almighty, He will raise you to be victorious.

Jeremiah 33:3 "Call to me and I will answer you and tell you great and unsearchable things you do not know."

Chapter 25

Prayer Can Change Things

Throughout the toughest and even the happiest moments of your life don't forget to pray. Don't be ashamed or shy to pray, and most importantly don't be proud to pray, because prayer has the ability to change your life. You may or may not agree with me but prayer has the power to move mountains.

I remember what my situation was and only through prayer did those situations change. The people in my life said I wouldn't achieve anything in life. And yet it was through prayer that I was able to overcome all that.

The best part about prayer is that it is available to anybody at any given time. God is never too busy to listen to you. He is the one who created you and the reason for that is for you to converse and speak to Him. And He would love to speak to you anytime. There are times I speak to Him, even when I don't need anything. The reason is simple: when I do need Him, I don't need to introduce myself.

Let's be honest, you'll never be able to make it without God. If you've tried it, see how far have you've gone. You need God. I have needed Him at every step of my life. You need to tell Him as well that you need Him. Don't be ashamed of telling your creator. He made you and also gave you the desires of your heart.

He is more than happy to hear your call and even answer your desires. He has made it possible for me to reach where I am. Prayer can make wonders happen in your life. I would also add that never has a prayer of mine gone unanswered. It has taken time for me to build my faith. And when the time was right all that I asked for was given. Hence I'm sharing with you this message that saved my life and helped me attain great heights. I came across this while I was a kid. "I'm just a nobody, trying to tell everybody, about somebody that can save everybody, and that's Jesus."

Be grateful for what you have; you'll end up having more. If you concentrate on what you don't have, you will never, ever have enough.

- Oprah Winfrey

Chapter 26

Learn To Be Grateful

Is it necessary to be grateful? And what should I be grateful for, is what you may be wondering. When you recollect the things you are grateful for it's like announcing the things God has already blessed you with. This will in some way or the other boost your spirit and provide you with the strength to march forward.

When I'm hustling and come across roadblocks that don't seem to move, I get restless. No matter what age or stage of life I am at, I'm human too and it's normal to face this. I keep a diary of things I have been blessed with at this young age. And believe me, God has been really generous with His grace on me. I wouldn't have been alive without His unfavoring grace. I did not dream of writing a book, or delivering speeches and hosting weddings. It's all by Him.

When you list the things that you've been blessed with, you proclaim the talents, the positions, the love, and the people that the Almighty God has been generous with in your life. It helps you realize all the turmoils your life has gone through and how you've survived all that. Hence, list down everything and place it in a place you pass regularly. Do not keep it in a storeroom that you visit once in many years. Counting your blessings helps you relive and helps build the belief that you will get through any challenge. It will help nurture a feeling that will make you feel blessed.

No matter if you fail or succeed at what you do. Just be grateful that you have the courage, spirit, and willingness to go through this, because only a few can withstand this.

My Learnings

Sometimes life gives you a second chance, or even two! Not always, but sometimes. It's what you do with those second chances that counts.

- Dave Wilson

Chapter 27

Life Gave Me A Second Chance

In my life I have been very fortunate to move away from the destructive ways I had chosen during my early days. As mentioned in the earlier chapters I used addictive substances, but after breaking those chains and setting myself free I never looked back towards that path. But not everyone is lucky to break those bonds of captivity. That God gave me two second chances is what I'm most thankful for.

The first one was walking away from drugs and living a clean life. The second instance was when I had to leave my parents' residence at 19 and had nowhere to go. I still remember how things were for me. And in moments like these, when I was completely broken with no one ready to shelter me from my family, help came from my aunt Maria Pontes. She asked me whether I would be comfortable staying at her place. In spite of being a single mom, going through a tough time in her relationship with my uncle, my dad's elder brother, she decided not to think about what others would say and just went with her heart's instinct.

It was the roughest patch of my life. I didn't speak much to people and remained in a cocoon. I remember one day my aunt and my sister, Gail, talking to me and telling me not to stay trapped by the things that had happened to me. They urged me to let those moments go and reminded me that there was more to life. My aunt encouraged me saying staying weak was not going to help me. But going out there and proving myself right with massive success would change everything. She told me not to react to the haters and focus on my journey and destination. She advised me not to get caught up in justifying myself to the world as they didn't deserve it. They emboldened me to remember that the future belongs to me and depended on how I shaped it.

There were many hateful comments, taunts and even abuses thrown at me. At times I was even sidelined at family events. Feeling ashamed in front of everyone I would try to avoid all gatherings. I was termed the black sheep of the family. I remember that after one event I broke down into tears on my way back home. I realized that anger and hatred towards them would lead me nowhere. And that not forgiving them was going to cost me. Because having unforgiveness is like you drinking poison and expecting the other person to die. I knew my time to reply had not come yet. Life sometimes takes its own time to reward you.

I just kept working hard, not with the intention of revenge but to improve my life. Hardwork is the only thing that pays off. My aunt, my sister, my then girlfriend and now wife Rochelle, and the Rodferntes family stood beside me through this tough times. I must add that Rochelle was my rock; she stood by me when I was dead broke and just had a vision. She supported my vision of what I wanted to do. I will never be able to pay any of them back for what they've done for me by accepting someone who was not their family and making me theirs. Accepting an unknown person and giving him a chance to build his life again.

At 22, I went to Singapore to study without a loan. The same year my wife and I bought a new house. When I came back I started to rebuild my business as an emcee. It took me four years to turn my tragedy into triumph. I started gaining popularity among the Catholic crowd for weddings and other social events. I could have used my first name as my stage name, but I chose to use my family name and go by Compere Pontes. My intention was to make the family name known and proud, irrespective of what my family thought. I knew they could badmouth my name but not the surname, I knew this would work in my favor. Slowly, word spread among my family friends about me and my work. By the grace of God I was hosting weddings and my network was growing. I had soon established myself in the market. Times had changed and the black sheep who was once rejected was now making the family name proud.

Today, I have made peace with my family, and somewhere I'm even thankful for the tough situations that have made me who I am. Life threw me an opportunity and I didn't stumble. If it hadn't been for the people who stood behind me I don't think I would have made it this far.

I've not written this chapter to gain sympathy, but to tell you that life will offer you chances to improve and make new things happen. How you respond to the call will decide the destiny of your life. It will determine whether you will move forward or fall backwards.

You call the shots and you make the decisions for your life. The power of positivity lies within you. Do not let bad situations cripple you. Instead, cripple the situation by not accepting defeat and staying down. Rise up and face the challenge head-on. I'd like to end this chapter with the words of Martin Luther King Jr., "Well, life for none of us has been a crystal stair, but we must keep moving, we must keep going. If you can't fly, run. If you can't run, walk. If you can't walk, crawl, but by all means, keep moving."

Sometimes God makes you cry
before He lets you roar.
                    - Sylvester Ryan Pontes

Chapter 28

You Will Be Crushed Before You Soar

Life is a journey, it introduces you to experiences that you would have never dreamed of. Surprises are a part of life, sometimes good and sometimes not so good. But I realized life is not complete without being crushed. Each one of us experiences a moment when you feel you have nothing left. You feel hurt, betrayed and lost. It's not without being crushed that you can soar. I'd like to share a chapter with you of my life. This event turned my life upside down. It was my crushing moment.

When I was 19, a beautiful thing happened to me; I met my girlfriend Rochelle. Just before that I had left all my addictions. Life was going absolutely fine and somehow I knew she was one for me. We wanted to take things slow as we were young and we wanted to focus on our careers as we were in our final year of graduation.

Now my parents weren't aware about this till a particular time. Some of you can relate to this, that some parents are detectives that can easily get a job at CIA or FBI. God knows how they got to know about it and from there started something I had never imagined I would ever go through.

When my parents found out that the girl I was dating wasn't from a family of supposedly equivalent status as ours, things started getting real difficult for me at home. There was a little less pressure from my dad, but my mom was raging against me every chance she got. Her anger was beyond control. She would do things that I can't explain in words. The taunts from her were so insulting and she would speak ill about my girlfriend each time there was a family gathering. My girlfriend had lost her parents at a very young age and she had to take care of her younger brother as her elder sister had just moved abroad for employment. We all know how hard it can get when there's no one to bring food to the family and you're struggling to make ends meet. My girlfriend's struggle made me reflect on the luxuries I had at home and made me feel blessed. She taught me to value money, which I used to spend rather carelessly before.

My mom tried everything to break us up, even spreading false tales to my girlfriend's brother. And things started getting really messed up after we started living together. Seeing that her efforts had no effect on me, on the morning of December 7, 2009, after a heated argument that led to a scuffle between me and my parents, I was asked to leave the house with whatever I had. I packed my clothes, my documents, my books from my graduation as I was in my final year. I remember they even made me sign out from certain financial documents. I can still remember that day. I had multiple bags in my hand and was crushed emotionally from within. I went from being part of a rich family to being thrown out on the streets. I remember I had 53 rupees in my pocket, no shelter, and no place to go.

This was the moment, I remember I was crushed to the core, broken in spirit. I immediately started calling friends to help me. No one returned my calls. I was on the streets as no family members were ready to house me or extend any help. I had my cousin, Gail, who I shared a great relationship with, and her mother, Maria, who I consider as my second mother. They invited me to live at their place with them. That's how I found shelter. Honestly, I feel, as the chapter says, you will be crushed before you soar. God actually puts you in these situations He makes you cry before you roar.

While I was living with my aunt, I had to take care of my basic necessities, as well as my college expenses, so I took up a job at a call centre. I worked the night shift and attended college in the mornings. It was difficult for me at the age of 20. But when life hits rock bottom the only way to go from there is up and higher. Rochelle and my aunt were my constant motivation. They wouldn't let me stay in pain but made me focus on the future. Rochelle and my aunt stood by me and I graduated from college with flying colors. I started working to collect money for higher education in Singapore. I must add I did my studies without a loan. While we were still dating, at the age of 22, Rochelle and I bought our own house.

Shortly after getting back from Singapore the emcee business started to pickup. I married the girl who stood beside me when I had absolutely nothing. And I must add we are immensely blessed and thankful to God. Today, the rejected Pontes family member has been accepted. But I feel no anger against them for what they did to me. If it hadn't been for Rochelle, Maria Aunty, Gail and the Rodferntes family who continuously backed me, pushed me to achieve things, and showered their love on me, nothing would have been the same.

When I reflect I wonder why this happened to me. What did I do wrong to go through such hardships. I found the answer, those whom God wants to anoint the most He crushes severely. The ones who God wants to exalt, He crushes the most, o that when He puts you at the top you don't become arrogant, but help other people who are at the same stage where you were. In order to extend the reach of an arrow, one had to pull it backwards so it can reach forward. Similarly, life drops you down so that you can rise and go further.

Take pride in just being yourself.
Be original.
                    - Sylvester Ryan Pontes

Chapter 29

Be The First You

This chapter was inspired by an event that occurred while I was hosting a wedding with one of the most energetic guests. I was engaged in conversation with guests and family members, when I was approached by a guest from the wedding.

He was a young guy who appreciated my work and was also aspiring to be an emcee. He asked me for tips on how to grow in this business as he had already hosted a few small events. After all the advice and the long conversation we had, he came up with a question which caught me off guard. He asked, "Sylvester, what advice would you give me if I wanted to become an emcee exactly like you?" My first thought was "Wow, what a compliment." I almost reached cloud nine but quickly came back to earth.

Now the question really stunned me. I could have answered anything to him, but I took a moment before replying. "Buddy, before you even try becoming the next me, try being the first you." I later explained to him, in simple terms, that the profession of a master of ceremonies is completely a people business. Whenever you perform you are constantly watched by the crowd. And people will automatically gauge if your delivery is original or fake. It's best to be yourself and not someone else. Because you can try imitating someone but you may never be able to duplicate the person. Be authentic to your core.

My message to everyone is to figure out what differentiates you from others. Make a note of those qualities, work on them, and create a niche in the market. Use those skills to dominate your sector and once you create a name in the business by being dedicated to it, you will grow in what you do.

"Be the first you" means be original as there is no gain in being somebody else. You are unique and there will never be another you. So take complete pride in just being yourself.

Always respect your audience and never take them for granted.
						- Sylvester Ryan Pontes

Chapter 30

Always Bring Your A Game

A master of ceremonies is always recognized by the crowd for his work, charm, energy, and elegance. One has to remember, they are only as good as their last show. And should treat their every performance like their last.

Sometimes, emcees take the crowd for granted and assume that either the crowd has low energy or the crowd number is thinned. Beware! I have come across situations where even the crowd that has the clumsiest-looking guests have left their seats and had a great time on the dance floor. They will surprise you to the core. You wouldn't know what just hit you. It can be demotivating when you expect a bigger crowd or are used to performing in front of large numbers and it turns out to be a small crowd. Bring your A Game to every show.

Never, never, never adjust your performance according to the size of the crowd. *It doesn't matter if you're speaking in front of a crowd of 40 or 40,000. Always respect your audience and never take them for granted.* And I say this from experience. You never know who in the crowd is watching you. You don't know who in that crowd of 40 may see your performance and offer you an opportunity that changes the whole trajectory of your life.

That one person could be The One with influence that can take you to a level you may never have imagined.

I experienced this while I was compèring an engagement for a Malyalee couple. As I entered the venue and saw the crowd my confidence dropped and I was thinking how I was going to do this. But as the fanfare started the crowd proved to be one of the most rocking crowds I've ever done an event for.

Here's the best part. In that crowd a lady was in search for a master of ceremonies for her son's destination wedding in Rajkot. I had never travelled beyond Mumbai and Goa for events at that time, but that woman gave me an opportunity to compere the wedding. Since that evening, things have changed for me for the better. Today, I get to travel to other countries as well; I am not restricted by boundaries. Within any crowd there may be one person who could help make your life soar like an eagle.

Become addicted to constant and
never-ending self-improvement.
- Anthony J. D'Angelo

Chapter 31

The Five D's Of Self Development

If you want to be great at anything, you have to be disciplined at it. Just like athletes practice daily, even years, before they reach their glory moment. It means you should be committed at improving yourself everyday.

Self development is a process. It's not a day's journey that can transform somebody from nothing to being something. It's a daily routine that pushes you and separates you from the rest. I'd like to share with you a process that worked for me and I'm sure will work for you as well. I realized that it takes five steps to start moving towards the life you always wanted to live. To get what you desire in life, you need to place your desires according to these five steps: Discover, Dream, Dedicate, Develop, and Design.

Discover: Discover the 'what' in your life that defines you. Figure out what makes your soul rejoice. Now that could be music, singing, painting, or simply any hobby dear to you. Each one of us has been made differently and so our interests will vary. But at any cost find your calling.

Dream: You have to envision yourself and see the future even before you start living it. Based on what you discover about yourself, what are you going to do differently than what you are doing now. See yourself doing on a bigger scale. For example, I used to dream about being on stage in front of so many people, even before I ended up being an emcee. Dream big so you can achieve bigger.

Dedicate: Once you're done with the part of dreaming, it's time to put your commitment in place. Dedication means come what may you're not going to step down from the commitment you made to yourself. It means you go all-in to achieve what you want. And do whatever it takes to get there.

Develop: Develop, in this context, means how you sharpen your sword. Undertake tasks to get better at what you plan to do. When I started my journey as an emcee I would learn different techniques on how to keep the crowd engaged and how to deliver speeches. I would constantly find modules online to improve myself and strive to be the best.

Design: To reach a destination everyone needs a map. In the same way, to lead your life in the direction you want, you need to draw a path. Treat that path as a GPS system to the destination you want to reach. Make sure there are no shortcuts to it. Push yourself with full force. And remember, while on the journey you designed don't stop till you reach the top.

By just keeping these five pointers in my mind I was able to achieve what I desired. I'm sure this will be a simple guide for each one of you. My best wishes to all who would dare to walk the path towards their destination.

Don't strive to be famous, strive to be effective and of value.
                        - Sylvester Ryan Pontes

Chapter 32

Impact Lives — Make A Difference

The most selfish thing you can ever do in your life is to not help someone else. When you do, there is a feeling beyond description that when you feel. A joy in your heart that is greater than any prized possession on earth. To see someone else excel in life with your assistance makes you a game changer in someone's life.

When you make it through the tides and reach the peak, where you always desired to be, I want you to remember my words. Go back down and pull someone else up to where you are. Keep doing this and slowly you will start experiencing a feeling that money can't buy. Don't aspire to get rich and acquire possessions, aspire to make a difference in others' lives.

I have often noticed, it's common human behavior for people to try to be famous in the crowd by showing off their work and popularity. It may suit some, but my advice is not to be famous, but be effective and of value. Do not help someone with the intention of being famous and gathering people's attention. All these things lead to self pride. Offer help with the intention of not receiving anything in return. And what you have done in silence God will reward you for.

Possessions and positions will always only be here on earth; you can't take them with you. But your contribution in changing people's lives will be the reason you will be remembered for generations. Each one of us has been placed on earth for a purpose. I found my purpose, to inspire people to find their calling. My prayer is that you are able to do the same, and find your true calling.

Being selfish will take you nowhere.
 - Sylvester Ryan Pontes

Chapter 33

Be The Giver

It is said that charity starts from home but my idea of giving here is to cultivate the habit of giving to others.

The Bible says, *"Whoever sows sparingly will also reap sparingly, and whoever sows generously will also reap generously. Each of you should give what you have decided in your heart to give, not reluctantly or under compulsion, for God loves a cheerful giver."* 2 Corinthians 9:6-7

The scripture above speaks about sharing with a joyful heart. And that is what we are called to do. We have been taught since childhood to share with our friends and family. Every child has been taught this at home and school. But as we grow as adults we tend to allow the quality of selfishness into us. And let me tell you that this is a common thing among humans, and I'm no exception.

But over the years I have learned that sharing of knowledge and ideas with others who lack or are unaware of it has helped me grow as an individual. Knowing something and being of help to others to grow at their skill is the best thing. Knowledge kept to oneself is a waste if not shared or multiplied, in my opinion.

Sometimes, sharing what we know helps us to learn more. We all constantly in a learning stage and never has anyone lost out by sharing what he's got. I'd like to suggest a small deed you can do. When you reach the destination you have always wanted to be in life, you're at the top of the pinnacle. Take a look down and you will see someone who are still struggling to make it to the top. When you see such people show them the way by trying to free them from their sticky situation and help them prosper. There is a lot of joy in doing this. Creating another success, like you, by helping someone, without the expectation of receiving anything in return is the best thing you can ever do for anyone.

Monetary help is not the help everyone is looking for; sometimes they need direction and confidence to walk on their path. The ones you help with your experience will always be grateful. Make a difference with your gift so that others do the same with theirs. The more you give back to society the more you shall receive. The talent or gift you posses should be your medium to share and make a difference in others' lives.

After all of my experiences I have learnt that givers gain.

Everything in life is a sale and
everything you want is a commission.
                                    - Grant Cardone

Chapter 34

Sell Like A Genius

Sales is a word that many people run from. Some may say it is not for them. But if I said your whole life depends on it would you believe it? Selling is the single most important thing that helped me grow my talent and take it to different levels that changed my life. I cannot imagine what I would do without knowing how to sell.

Selling is a prerequisite for all the success you will create for yourself in this world. Regardless of your career or what you do, selling impacts every person on this planet. And you can't run away from it. Your ability or inability to sell, persuade, influence, negotiate, and convince others will affect every area of your life. It will determine the course of your life.

Regardless of who you are or what position you hold, whether you're the CEO, HR, janitor, accountant, or postman you will have to sell to others what you believe in. No one is excluded from selling. You will have to convince others about your dreams at some time or the other.

But here, I'm not talking about selling products, I'm talking about selling yourself and others on those things you want in your life. I'd like to share an example with you. Imagine if you had the best talent in the market, for instance painting. And you realize that you're the best painter in your country, better than anybody in the market. But when it comes to selling your paintings or describing the images to the buyer your voice goes silent trip. That changes the whole ball game or you. Suddenly you lose the upper hand in what you're good at. Having talent is good but not having the complementary skill to sell that talent will frustrate you over a period of time. The ability to get people to like you, like your work, and even to make them hire you is all about selling. The number one sales trainer on earth, Grant Cardone says, "Sales is not a job but a way of life."

Many people come up with great and innovative ideas everyday. But they lack the ability to sell those ideas to the market to get people to invest in them. No entrepreneur can build a business without understanding this critical element called sales.

Whatever you do in life, learn everything about sales, because your life and your dreams depend on it.

I don't care about what people think
or say about me, I know who I am.
                        - Jonathan Davis

Chapter 35

Don't Care What People Think

We are almost always preoccupied with what others think. This is the number one reason why most people step back from achieving greatness. They start on their journey to get where they want to be and then turn back halfway. We live in a society surrounded by people — family, friends, and acquaintances. Some of these we hold close to our heart and some we don't.

We sometimes curb our actions according to the people we are spending time with. This could be because we want to please them or else they have built up a perception about you. Spoiler alert: When you try pleasing others, you displease yourself.

I am sure you must have come across this in life, when you might have liked the idea of a particular career and you were convinced it was the right one for you. Then one day you decided to run this by your family or maybe a friend. Instead of the person motivating you to go ahead and pursue it, they come back at you with negativity and horror stories of how many people had failed before you. They give you their expert advice without having any experience in that field. That's why I have termed negative people as the biggest dream killers.

Some may have given up on their dreams and will urge you to join the bandwagon. This is quite normal these days; one loser will always want to recruit someone new. It is observed that if you hang around with five losers, you become the sixth. So it's very important to eliminate the negativity and focus on what you want. Because no matter how hard you try to convince others about your dream they will never understand.

Let me share a small anecdote. When I had just started as a master of ceremonies I was completely sold on the idea. This was what I wanted to pursue. I saw myself as an entertainer. I could see myself on the stage. I was so excited I told my mom about it. To my surprise she said something I never expected. She said no one would want to hire a master of ceremonies who was so short. She said emcees were usually tall and I should give up this idea. She told me to stop wasting time and concentrate on something worthwhile.

This coming from my mother, I thought she knew more about me and would want the best for me. Then, negative thoughts started crowding my mind. What she said was true. At five feet three inches, I wasn't tall at all. All the other anchors I had seen were closer to six feet in height and I would be a midget among them. To add to that, I was also the shortest in my family. I was about to give in, but something from within didn't want to surrender to this thought.

I remember I really wanted to pursue this, but in the absence of support, my self-confidence was taking a hit. I had a burning desire to be on stage and my dream was on the line. I decided not to care about what my family thought or said about me. I decided to go against their will and just do it. I didn't fear the results because if I failed at it I wouldn't regret not trying. I worked hard on it and refused to hear any negative comments from anyone about it. As time went by I started taking up shows and learnt and improved my stage skills. Close to a decade later, I have never thought about looking back.

It is very important that you ***don't let anyone's opinion about you end up becoming your destiny.*** In spite of my mother discouraging me I did what I believed in. I know it can be hard when you have to go against your loved ones, but just because others don't get your vision, doesn't mean it is not important.

I believe that dreams are an idea and how you add fuel to it through your action brings it to reality. When you add no action to your dreams they go with you to your grave. Imagine this morbid scene: you are on your deathbed and you see all the potential dreams you could have brought to life, but you didn't because you were busy taking others opinions. Don't let it happen to you. Even the Almighty would be disappointed with you for not using and multiplying the gifts that He handed over to you. You have one life and one chance to make it big. So disregard what negative people say or think and just go ahead and do what your heart says. Trust me, you shall live life as a happy soul.

Words can inspire, words can destroy.
Choose yours well.
                                    - Robin Sharma

Chapter 36

Power Of Words

As a speaker or emcee your biggest strength is the words that you use. It may not be your vocabulary necessarily but the way to present your thoughts to the audience. It's important to assess what you will speak because words are like weapons. They can set the mood for an amazing evening or spoil it. It can make an audience go wild or put them to sleep. Words are an individual's strongest tool that can be used as his sword.

Words when used and articulated in the right way can influence people. It can change people's beliefs. You may want to deliver a statement to appreciate something really beautiful, but if you use the wrong words to describe it, you will definitely create a mess. How you deliver your words out to the crowd determines how they will receive your information. Over the years words have been used to motivate people for greater tasks many times positively and sometimes otherwise.

Martin Luther King Jr. and Adolf Hitler are two leaders the world has witnessed. Apart from being great leaders of their time and excellent orators, each had the ability to attract huge crowds. If you analyze their lives you'll find out how they used their words in speeches so constructively that when they finished the crowds would go wild.

Martin Luther King Jr. fought for equality for black people and although he was the victim he spoke words of glory, love, and hope. That things would change and how each person could contribute to bringing change. His words would encourage people in distress to believe and dream for a new day.

On the other hand, Hitler's words were vicious venom, aggravating his audience. His words motivated the army and people to hate and increase the atrocities against his enemies. He was one of the very few people in history who influenced his audience and infused fear into their minds at the same time, with the use of a single weapon, his words.

These examples, although extreme, are enough for you to decide what path you would like to choose as an individual. If you are hosting a social function or a speaking engagement no matter, as long as you are in charge of the microphone it's your responsibility to be cautious and courteous. It's only what you say and how you say it that leaves an imprint in the minds of the people. What you say is what people identify you with. Your words can act as a double-edged sword. Always use them positively, because words once spoken cannot be taken back.

I'd like to end this chapter with a lines from Mohammed Qahtani, "Words are power. Words could be your power. You can change a life, inspire a nation and make this world a beautiful place. Your mouth can spit venom, or it can fix a broken soul." Use your words to create a difference and positive impact that helps in changing lives.

It is better to aim high and miss
than to aim low and hit.
- Les Brown

Chapter 37

My Biggest Mistake — Aiming Too Low

As humans, we all make mistakes. But making mistakes and not learning from them is a crime. I'm about to share the biggest mistake of my life. And you may agree with me or not on this, but I suggest you do not commit the same mistake.

Ever since I made a commitment to myself to live a life of abundance, I had set my list of goals with a determination to get me where I wanted to be. And so I listed them according to what I thought I could achieve.

Denzel Washington said, "Dreams without goals remain dreams and fuel disappointment." So have dreams and have life goals.

After I moved out of my parents house, things weren't on my side. I had barely enough money, no shelter, and my back against the wall, until I got shelter at my aunt's place.

We all set goals in life. Students set the percentage they want to achieve in an exam, college grads set their idea of a good job, a young man or woman sets the age they want to get married. Some have small goals, while others have large ones. Some may be related to life and some may have to do with wealth. It is always great to set goals, and I did the same.

While I was caught up in the things I did right, I missed out on the most important part about it. I was lucky enough to find out that quickly that what I was aiming for was my biggest downfall.

I had learnt that one needed to define life goals to achieve. You can't move forward when the road is confused and foggy.

So I religiously followed this and wrote down my goals. I wanted: to own at least three houses in Mumbai, write a book on my life, reconcile with my family, own a restaurant, get famous on Facebook, and have a certain amount of money in my bank account.

I worked hard and strived to achieve my goals, but when I came close to them I failed. It took time for me to realize where I had gone wrong. That's when reality struck and I found that my biggest mistake was I had aimed too low.

When you have goals that are small, your effort in achieving them remains small. Your game plan in reaching there and the action taken to achieve it is small. And all you get from it is dissatisfaction. The whole ball game changes when you shift your aim a bit higher and set humongous goals.

I want you to think on these lines. Imagine if you have set a realistic goal of making 50 thousand a year versus five million in a year. Do you think it will take the same amount of effort to make five million that it takes to make 50k?

The answer is no. But what it does is make you sad. Failing on a bigger goal is much better than failing on a small one. Just like if you aim at five million and hit three million, it is better than aiming at 50k and missing.

I urge each one of you, when you make your goal list, make sure your goals are big. Your goals should be so big that your problems melt in front of them. They should be so huge that people mock you for having such big dreams. And they will only mock you as they can't match your thinking capacity. When people see your goals being completely beyond reach, you will be called words like arrogant, greedy, highly ambitious. I have gone through this a lot of times, sometimes from my near and dear ones.

Be silent, stay focused, and let your success shut them up once and for all. Remember, you can fake many things in this world, but you can never fake success to the world. One of the things that I have learned is that success often comes to those whose goals and dreams are bigger than the rest. So aim higher!

If you have to choose between a good reputation and great wealth, choose a good reputation. (Proverbs 22:1)

Chapter 38

Build Character And Reputation

We all agree that money is very important for everyone to survive. Nobody wants to be in a situation where they don't have any money. To be honest, the profession of a master of ceremonies is a rewarding one both in terms of recognition and money. Similarly, there are other interests and arts that are equally attractive in terms of money. The thing about money is that sometimes it can give rise to greed and cause humans to make mistakes, as everybody loves making money, including me. However, *in the process of making money be conscious not to make the wrong move to attain it.*

The reason I choose to add this topic in the book is because it's important. Sometimes, we may or may not notice it in our daily lives, but I have come across instances where I have witnessed people letting go of their conscience in the lust of acquiring money in an inappropriate manner. In the world the most important thing you can earn is goodwill and a good reputation for your name. That is the most precious jewel one can own, apart from having pots of money. And there is a thin line to maintaining your reputation among others.

Whatever you do, whether a job, business, or any task it reflects a part of your character. My advice is to put your complete heart into what you do. If you're a dishwasher, be the best at it. If you fix cars or are a mechanic, be the best at it. Be the best at what you do. Be so good at what you do that when someone thinks about making a decision your name should be at the top of their mind.

Happy customers wont be able to live without your services.
- Marley Majcher

Chapter 39

Don't Surprise Your Clients — Amaze Them

You may be wondering why I added two words that are almost synonymous in the title. Well, if you ponder a little you will realize that there is a subtle difference between these words. Surprise means to catch someone completely off guard. Amaze, one the other hand, means you do something that is way beyond their expectations.

Everyone, irrespective of whatever field they are in, is always keen to satisfy their clients and peers. If you're given a task, you would look forward to getting it done and be relieved from that duty. But have you considered that if you added just a little more effort to that task, the outcome could be completely mind-boggling?

To do this is not a day's effort, it requires dedication, desire, a strong will, and focused mindset. We, as humans, tend to lose concentration halfway through a task, no matter how motivated we were when we started. To stand out from others in any profession, one must be ready to evolve and change their ways. It requires a daily grind and the desire to evolve into something you never were. No matter what profession or business you are in, we are called to be radiant and to make a difference to people's lives.

Here are three questions you must ask yourself every day:

How can I grow?

What can I give?

What can I celebrate?

How can I grow?

To deliver beyond expectations one must be ready to push beyond his own limits, growing a little each day. If you ask yourself how you can grow every day just add a new learning to your life each day. In just a year's time your life will be different from the one you are living currently. If you practice this daily, in just 365 days, you will evolve so radically that even you'll be astounded by the results.

What can I give?

It is said that the more you give the more you gain. Whatever you do in life, give your best at it. Whatever little you add — be it effort, time, or even a kind word — can work wonders. It is my belief that when you share your knowledge, you gain the most. We all are gifted with talents. How we use those talents to glorify the Almighty who gifted it, is in our hands. Don't always expect a return on what you share because having an expectation in return is selfish. Be sure of this: what you give unto others with a clear heart will always return to you in mysterious ways and with abundant blessings.

What can I celebrate?

Once you start evolving as a person by constantly learning every day and sharing your learning with others, the result may not come forth right away. Your greatest gift will be the testimony of people whose lives you've touched in your lifetime. And that's what adds real meaning to celebrating your journey in this world as a person who gave everything and received his blessings tenfolds.

If you want to kill a dream, share it
with someone who hasn't got one.
                        - Sylvester Ryan Pontes

Chapter 40

How To Kill A Dream

I'm writing this chapter so that you don't make the same mistakes I've made in my life. I know how it feels when you discover what your course of life should be and the joy that fills your heart at that moment. Now all that is good, till you share your dream and revelation with someone who doesn't think like you or isn't goal-oriented.

That's what I did, I shared my thoughts with people who were close to me. Now just because they were close to me doesn't mean they shared the same vision I did for my life. With that followed the journey of self-doubt that they raised in my mind. "It's not possible, you can't do it, don't dream too big, you won't go that far." These were the words I came across when I decided what I wanted to do.

That's when I realized that, **if you want to kill a dream, share it with someone who hasn't got one.** Because the vision you received for your life is not the same revelation for others. And by sharing it others you gives them the opportunity to burden you with all the negative thoughts and failures of their lives. The world is a cruel place with people who will pull you down. And honestly you don't need that crap at all.

Do not invest your time sharing your dreams with others. Use that time to develop, create, and work on a plan to get you to where you want to be.

To expect the unexpected shows a
thoroughly modern intellect.
- Oscar Wilde

Chapter 41

Expect The Unexpected

Life is a roller-coaster with ups and downs. Events that you may foresee coming or not. It is usually said that if you knew what's in the future for you, life wouldn't be that exciting. Hence, certain events or situations arise to shape the course of our thinking and life.

I'm talking from my experiences of being an emcee, but this chapter can be related to other aspects of life too. As an emcee, you are the head of the event. No matter how prepared you are, you should always be ready to face unforeseen circumstances that can erupt anytime either before, during, and sometimes even after the event. Always have your head straight on your shoulders and have a calm mind. Don't hit the panic button. You are the first line of defense for the client. If you don't hold your ground, the outcome of the event is going to be dreadful.

You may have a Plan A. But you need to always improvise it when a crisis situation arises. Bring your best artillery, take control, and make the change. Times like these will bring out the best within you. It's in these moments your talent and art are put to test. How you react to the situation determines what the outcome will be. Every move you make can either be the one that glorifies you and saves the day or the one that changes the whole horizon of the event.

Never run from the action scene — face it! Trust me, *the show never ends in these situations, it just changes its dimension. If you do something that will change or impact people's lives they will remember you till eternity.* I have faced many moments like these and each time I come across a new challenge, it is always a learning experience for me. And I always pray that everything goes smoothly. But you just don't know what's going to happen next. Believe me, when you overcome situations like these it completely redefines you as a master of ceremonies. Always accept these events as a gift and opportunity from God as your moment to shine. Your reward for this will always be in the form of loud chants and applause from the crowd. And this I bet, you shall cherish that moment forever.

I'm now sharing a crisis situation that came my way. I hope they help you think outside the box.

I hosted my college mate's wedding in Mumbai in December 2017. The planning that went into this wedding was tremendous, with both sides excited. We had the most electrifying crowd an emcee could ask for and everyone was set to have a ball of a time. The groom, my friend, was from Mangalore and the bride was from Goa. Everything was going absolutely smooth right from the entrance, slicing of the cake, toast, wedding march, and first dance. Everyone was busy on the dance floor having a great time. In Mangalorean weddings, there is a tradition where the bride changes from the white wedding gown to the traditional *saddo* (a red sari). Now, usually, the time limit for open-air weddings in Mumbai is 10 pm. There are restrictions on sound after that.

Around 9:25 pm, the bride was getting ready to enter the venue again in her *saddo*. I had escorted the couple to the entrance and was just heading to coordinate with the DJ and to alert the crowd that the bridal couple was ready to enter again. As I headed to the DJ corner, which was 200 meters from the entrance, I caught sight of the crowd dancing and having a good time. Then suddenly BOOM!!! The lights went out. I checked my watch. It was 9:30 pm. I don't need to tell you how crowds react when the electricity goes off suddenly. It was pitch dark, and all I could hear was the sound of people trying to find each other and family members panicking. The DJ and I looked at each bewildered. Never in my life had I come across such a situation and I wasn't prepared for something like this. Moreover, it was my friend's wedding and I didn't want it to go down this way. I had to do something that would turn things around and soon. The clock was ticking and we had a few other things pending on the to-do list too.

Action plan: The first thing that I did was to calm the family members and the guests. I myself didn't know what the issue was, but I told them it was under control and we would take care of it. (Note: Never leave your crowd in a panic state. Stand by them. You do not need people going frantic. Because if they do, it becomes an impossible situation to control.)

The next step was to find the guy responsible for the electricity. I got in touch with him and asked him how long it would take for the lights to come back on. (Note: Never get into an argument when you're in a situation; it will only add fuel to the whole issue. Always look for a solution instead of someone to blame.) The decor vendor said he would need 15 minutes to get the lights on. By the time I ran back to the DJ's corner, I heard the best man trying to arrange candles so that the couple could enter. That is a good idea, but also could get dangerous. (Note: Never let the situation go out of your hand. Take control).

In the midst of all this, I had an idea that changed the whole dimension of the evening. It came to me while I was roaming the whole ground with the torch from my cell phone. I quickly ran to all the four ends of the quadrangle and shouted on top of my voice asking the guests to turn on their cell phone flashlights and get ready to welcome the couple. The guests did exactly that, and with enthusiasm. Waving their cell phone flashlights, they made the venue look like a field full of fireflies. Later, the lights came back and guess what?! The people absolutely loved the flashlight bit. In fact, most of them thought the whole thing was staged by the couple. This was one of the most memorable moments I have had in my years of anchoring weddings.

PS: For the video of the event, please refer to my YouTube Channel: Pontes Sylvester.

Barriers You Need to Overcome

There is no illusion greater than fear.
- Lao Tzu

Chapter 42

Conquer Fear

The questions I get asked most often are: Don't you fear the crowd and the stage? What if you forget what you were going to say? Or what if someone interrupts you and you lose track?

Well, honestly speaking, I am no Superman and I always feared these situations. In fact, at times, I almost wanted to quit. But when I take a step back and think about it now, I must say it really doesn't help.

As time progressed I learned that if you don't know how to do a particular task and to master it try doing it badly over and over and your effort at doing it will always be different. Also, in the process, every action you take will help you to do that thing better. When the question of fear arises, I tell people the full form of 'FEAR' is False Events Appearing Real. And this is what I learned from Les Brown and Grant Cardone.

Fear is nothing but your subconscious mind taking control and assuming the outcome, which is not real. Since childhood, our minds are filled with thoughts such as don't do this, don't do that. The amount of "don't do" we hear in our childhood is so jarring that each time there is an event that will push us beyond our capacity, our subconscious mind is programed to step in and try to save you from taking action. And if you don't reprogram your mind into reverse thinking you will always be caught in this trap.

The best way is to overcome fear of the stage, for instance, is to get on stage. If you won't try anything, how would you know you will fail. I've learnt this from a video I watched of Mel Robbins and it really helped me boost my confidence. She says that each time there is a negative thought or an idea that crosses don't let it reside there. The trick that works to overcome this negativity is very simple. Close your eyes and count backwards from five to one. This five-second window helps you retrain your brain and mind to start anew. Remember, the more you let the thought thrive in your mind the more damage you are doing to yourself. I use the backwards counting tip every time I wander into negative thoughts. Before I end this chapter, I must confess: sometimes, no matter how positive or well prepared I am, there are moments when I still have a tiny bit of fear within me that leaves me restless. That's when I recite these words of God from the Bible. It has never failed me at any time or any stage of my life. It's from the book of Isaiah Chapter 41:10: *"Do not fear, for I am with you. Do not be dismayed for I am your God. I will strengthen you and help you. I will uphold you with my righteous hands."* This is my one secret weapon. And now it is yours.

Never mind what haters say. Ignore
'em 'til they fade away.

- T.I.

Chapter 43

How To Handle Criticism

Handling criticism is one of the most interesting areas of any business. Some clients will praise you and some will call you a disgrace. Some criticism is constructive and some can be destructive. Some will please you, and some will literally make your blood boil. One thing is for certain: in the business, you can't please everyone and you shouldn't even try.

How you act in a situation determines whether or not you will dominate the outcome. Most of us, including me, have come across criticism, and to be honest there are times I didn't really know how to handle it. *I have succumbed to defeat in life and business. It's not about how many times you fail, it's what you learn each time you fail.*

I have always accepted positive comments with a smile and when the negative ones came, I welcomed them with an even broader smile.

Most people wonder and are afraid of negatives. I'm of the opinion that criticism is someone's opinion — let's respect it not try to justify it. That cuts the negativity right there.

Channel the negativity into your business positively. How do you do that? It's very simple. For example, it's human nature to glorify others' bad habits or doing.

Look at it this way, one satisfied customer will praise you in front of 100 people, but a dissatisfied customer will negatively preach about you to 1000 people and more. Every corner of the globe the person goes to, he will spit your name in front of others even if they really are not connected.

The outcome: More people now know you than before. It doesn't matter what they think if they know you personally or not. Sometimes, you just need the haters to do the marketing for you.

In business, always remember *If people don't know you, they won't do business with you. That's the bottomline.* I have come across so many criticisms in my career and in my life that it doesn't really matter now. I just use them to my benefit. *If your work speaks to the crowd, the loudmouths shut up after a while automatically.*

PS: At any point, don't let anyone's criticism towards you lead to hatred in your heart. That will be victory to them and self-defeat.

No pressure, no diamonds.
                    - Thomas Carlyle

Chapter 44

Resist The Pressure

You are often surrounded with a lot of noise around you, clatter that doesn't matter. This is the reason why and how we go astray. In spite of knowing what our vision is, we get driven away and often disheartened when the results don't go as planned. Though we invest all our sweat and blood into it things move very slowly.

I'm sure each one of us can relate to what I'm talking about. But do you stay focused and keep your head on your shoulders when things are just not going right? When situations don't go as planned, how do you keep the fuel and fire burning? Times like these are reasons for dreams to be killed or fulfilled.

Moments like these are testing times for you and your dreams. And trust me, it's hard to hang on and easy to just let go, while you battle these moments of your life. Let me tell you that situations like this have made many weak, and even led them to crumble. It's the strong minds that endure through the struggle and make it to the top. It's the attitude of how you handle and view the situation that decides the outcome. Whether the pressure bends you or vice versa. Keep in mind, tough times don't last but tough people do. While you are sailing through the low tides of your life, are you going through it or are you growing through it?

Because your attitude towards the situation decides the outcome of your situation.

My advice is to increase your efforts by 10 times, push harder and find the reason you started in the first place to fuel you. Sometimes going back to the initial purpose helps reignite your mind and gives you a kickstart.

While you're at your grind even in the most desperate situations, when all that matters to you is on the line, the word 'quit' should not come to your mind. The situation will bow down to your resilience and tenacity and fall in your favor. Even God favors the bravehearted. So fear not the situation in front of you, fear the magnitude of your success once you overcome it. And let success be the reason for you to resist, reclaim, and reach your destination.

Refuse to lose, and you shall
find a way to win.
                    - Sylvester Ryan Pontes

Chapter 45

Be Persistent And Tenacious

We all have faced failure in the beginning of whatever we have decided to do. And it makes us feel miserable. But in order to excel and be victorious you've got to be persistent. You're going to come across small failures and big failures through your journey. People will either hate you or be barriers in your journey. But at all times keep your head up and eyes on the goal. Move forward and these instances will make you better. The steps or action you take after those moments of your life will help you get better results.

So you can commit to going through that process or you can look at someone else some years down the line and say man that guy got lucky. Don't feel ashamed if you fall down in your effort to reach where you want to be. Retrain your mind to talk yourself back into getting to your goal. Only feel ashamed if you quit on your grind.

Be persistent and tenacious and think about the reward at the end of the struggle. Remember the time, effort, blood, and sweat invested by you. Just as you're getting close to hitting that jackpot are you going to surrender? I know it may certainly not be easy for your body and mind to carry on, but gather courage from your heart and march on. These small steps of courage and resilience will lead you to open doors.

It is alright to fail, but a crime
to stay a failure.
- Sylvester Ryan Pontes

Chapter 46

Failure Is Good, But Don't Let It Fail You

We are all bound to fail at some point or the other on our journey to success. But the key is to not let that failure fail you. This idea carries a deep meaning. In life we aspire for many things; we have many dreams and desires. Our attempts may lead us to go to the extreme limits in order to achieve these goals. And in spite of all these efforts there are times when things don't go as planned because many situations may not work as per your desire. Failure comes your way and breaks your hope, your fighting spirit, and your desire.

In times like these how you handle your failure plays a very important role. How is your attitude during your failure or downfalls? Is failure something that breaks your momentum, or does it give you the strength to accelerate? Do you quit and let go of your dreams, or do you stand up gather the left pieces of you and start marching back on the same track?

I remember this dialogue from the Sylvester Stallone movie *Rambo* where he says, "Life will hit you hard many times, but it ain't about how hard you hit, it's about how hard you get hit and keep moving forward."

I'd like to share a small part of my life here. As a kid I always wanted to study abroad. I wanted to learn about food, cooking, and the hotel industry. After graduating I continued working in the call center, but changed my profile to sales as the incentives would help me collect money for my education. I wanted to go to Switzerland for further studies. Having arranged for the initial payment and admission fees, my friend's dad and my aunt decided to help me out as guarantors for the bank loan. I asked my parents for small document, an identity proof. The bank had asked for this document as part of the paperwork. But my parents refused to help me out with it. In spite of me pleading, the answer from their end was a stern 'no'.

And that was how my Switzerland dream was shattered. I still remember how broken I was. I came close to achieving my dream and out of nowhere I lost it. Along with my shattered dream came another hit. I had to cancel my admission and so the college returned the fees after cutting a cancellation charge. Sometimes in life you try getting out of one problem only to walk into the next one. So was my situation. I had lost half of my savings and had to start all over again. Failure, however, has a way of making you stronger. It will break you at first, but also transform, heal, and harden you like a rock.

I had to gather the broken pieces and start building a new vision. I didn't lose sight of my dream. I was determined that I would study abroad, but this time without a loan and on my own. I started focusing my energy on my goal. I worked so hard that my incentives were five times more than my salary. I had to bring my best as I realized I had nothing to lose and everything to gain. That's why without losing my focus I completed my further studies in Singapore without a loan. And till today I cherish that moment of sweet victory.

Les Brown is one of the top five motivational speakers in the world. His famous quote always helps me to regroup and fightback. "When life knocks you down, try to land on your back. Because if you can look up, you can get up." Truly, I tell you, whenever life shows you failure, it is not to put you down. There could be something to learn from it. What attitude you display really will decide the outcome and the end result. Sometimes it's good to be tested by life as you would never know what you really are from within. These roadblocks are sometimes placed by God to set you up for something great and in accordance with His plan. He designs our journey so that we humans become a masterpiece and also an example to others.

You have greatness within you. As the Bible affirms in Philippians 4:13: *"I can do all things in Christ who strengthens me."*

As we are fearfully and wonderfully made in God's likeness, we are also instilled with the power to overcome failure and negativity and to be conquerors. Always celebrate failure, as you learn something from it. And if you treat life as journey of learning, then failure is just a part of the process. Accept that it is alright to fail, but a crime to stay a failure. At every stage of your journey in life God is using your experiences as a sculptor to chisel you into something marvellous. Because in the end, it's not over until you win.

Don't commit professional
suicide by doing something that
you are not interested in.
                    - Sylvester Ryan Pontes

Chapter 47

Let Your Purpose Motivate You, Not Money

There are many professions in the world that we are aware of, some may be doctors, engineers, pilots etc. Some may be highly paying jobs and some may not. Make sure that you don't end up choosing a career based on salary and not your interest. That is one of the biggest mistakes one can ever commit. Just because someone else is good at a particular task doesn't mean you will also be able to excel in that. The world is a much more creative place now, where creativity is glorified and has even found fame. Where professions in the olden days like engineers, doctors were respected in society, professions like musicians, singers, standup comedians are also given praise now. All these professions get well paid.

On a similar note, even the role of master of ceremonies is now one of the most respected professions globally. No matter how tedious and challenging the profession may be, it comes with a rewarding paycheck. An emcee usually also commands stature in society and popularity. It's a profession where, when you're at your peak, you can easily make a quick million.

Many get attracted towards professions that have a greater reward. Now don't get me wrong, though the money is good, if you don't put your heart right into the job, you won't get very far in any business. You really need to give your blood, sweat, and dedication to be a success in any profession. But before we get there it is very important to identify whether you are made for that profession. Does your interest lie in what you plan to do. ***Don't commit professional suicide by doing something that you are not interested in.***

You see in the title of the chapter I specifically mentioned this, because this is what matters most if you want to go from where you are to where you ought to be. If it's the money, fame, and attention you are hungry for in the profession or any line of work, then just don't do it. It's not worth doing something that will earn you a huge sum, because you will never learn and the money will restrict your learning curve. But when it's your passion then everything changes. Purpose will bring creativity in your work and at the same time will reflect your character in what you do.

It will lead you to the deepest corners of your heart and soul to bring out the best not only to satisfy your clients but also to go the extra mile beyond their expectations. Even after a decade, I still consider myself to be in a learning stage. Each event will teach you something you didn't know. That's how you perfect things and improve at every stage.

I have come across people during this span who are driven by money and the ones driven by passion. I have seen that people with passion and heart for the profession have often travelled more miles than the others.

If you want you can verify the facts for yourself. People like Bill Gates, Steve Jobs, Warren Buffet, Grant Cardone, Les Brown, Zig Ziglar, the Wright Brothers, Thomas Edison — all these inventors and businessmen came from humble beginnings. Some had a college education, but many didn't. But what brought them to where they are today is sheer determination and a strong passion for what believed in. They never quit. When you're driven by passion, you will always find success, regardless of failures along the way.

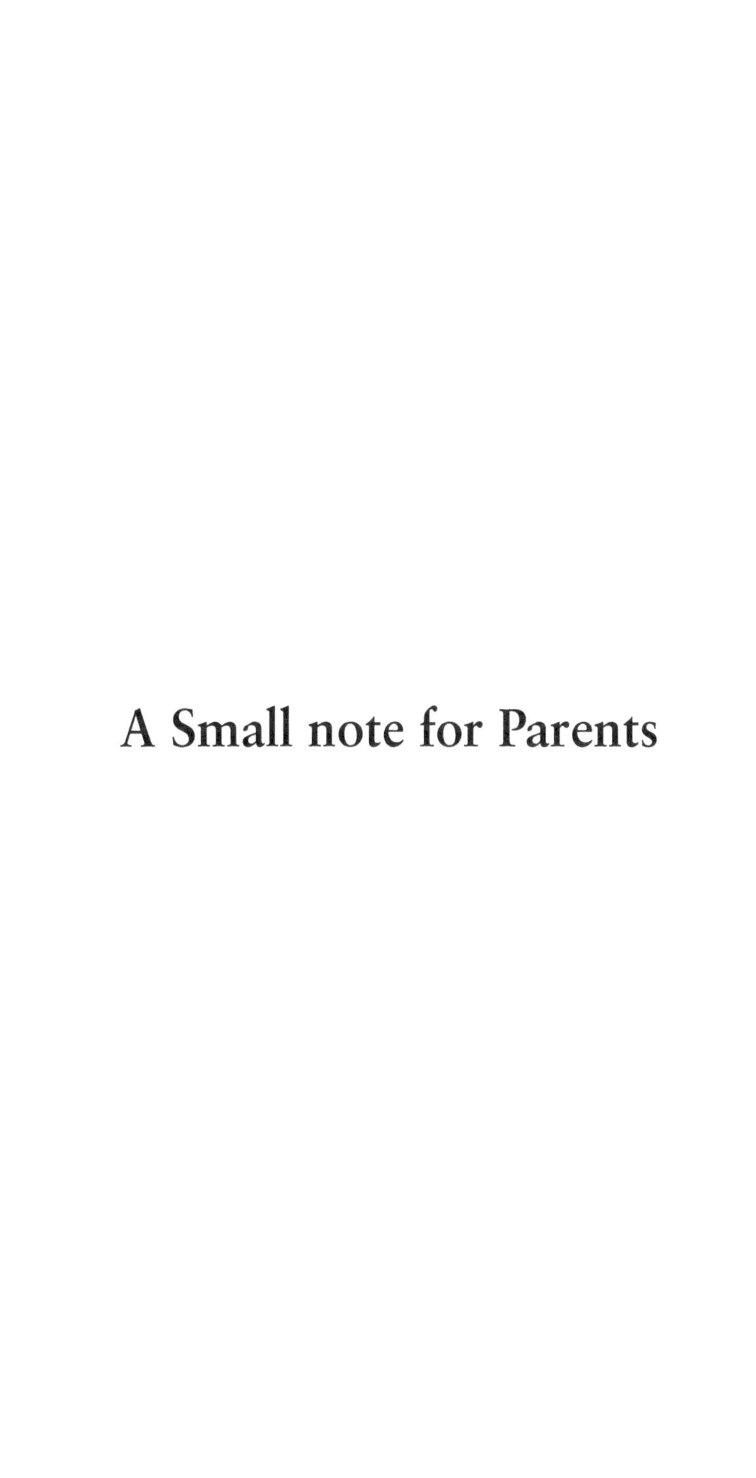

A Small note for Parents

We must teach our children to dream
with their eyes open.
- Harry Edwards

Chapter 48

Advice For Parents

It goes without saying that parents would always want the best for their kids. Till date I have never come across a parent who thinks otherwise. Take no offense by what I want to share in this chapter. It may be helpful and could relate to your life with your kids. But hear me out as it is something that really important — knowing your kid's heart and his or her gifts.

As parents, apart from the love we shower on our kids, we also start expecting results. As we live in a competitive society today, we tend to pressurize kids to score at examinations, sometimes to the extent of not settling for anything below 90. Thus pushing the kid to move up the academic ladder completely ignoring their creative side. Education is not the end of the world. That's why you can go to college and get a PhD and yet end up being broke. Every child has an expressive side, it could be art, singing, sports, etc. I'm not saying you should ignore academics, but only imposing academics and shunning the creative side is wrong.

This is a serious issue. I have come across kids losing their self-confidence and reaching a closed mindframe. They start doubting themselves, their dreams, their aspirations and start behaving in a completely introvert manner.

The saying, "All work and no play makes Jack a dull boy" is true. Do not force your kids to be robots when it's time for them to bloom. Instead, look patiently at their behavior. It is often at an early age that you can identify a path to his or her life. Watch their gifts closely and give them the opportunity to make their hobby a career.

Let me tell you that the education system is built to take your kid to a certain height or level, but remember, if your kids start following their gifts they will be unstoppable and the sky will be the limit for them to soar. Hence, my request to you, parents, is to be a lamp, and show your kids the way to their gift.

Take Action

Think, believe, dream and dare.
      - Walt Disney

Chapter 49

Dare To Make The Move

This chapter is for those who have gone through this book and have a gut feeling that there is something unexplainable within them is stopping them from achieving their share of greatness. I'm talking to you: let not the thought of fear stop you. If you have the fire and desire and have a story to tell the world, I encourage you and would like to tell you that you have greatness within yourself. Don't let it die within; let it flourish and multiply. If you have a dream, go for it with you heart and soul, sweat and blood. There will be hardships down the way but that will shape you and your life like a masterpiece. Don't let your dream go to the grave with you. Make it a reality today. Believe in yourself and the power you possess. It is remarkable and when used to its full potential, it will astonish you. Each time you reach a roadblock don't lose heart. Remember, you were put in that place at that moment only because God knows that you have the strength and resilience not only to face it but also to conquer it.

If you decide in your mind what you want, the universe will pull its forces together to make you receive it. If there is a voice within you, then there will always be a crowd waiting to hear that voice. Only time will decide when and how. And when that happens, it will be a feeling you may never be able to describe. This chapter is my attempt to put my point forward. I may or may not be able to make a huge difference or impact, but I'm sure these words of mine will spark the brain that will make the change. I'd like to share something that I read in a book and I totally believe it: "No matter what the situation, your dreams will always be yours, and if you fight for your dreams, your dreams will fight for you."

So, I dare you: take action and change your life. Who knows how much time you have left. Make the move!

Unleash the inner beast, do
whatever it takes.

- Anonymous

Chapter 50

Unleash The Beast Within

Each one of us has the voice of a warrior within us. Some of us explore it and some knowingly suppress it and frustrate not only ourselves but the people around us.

This voice within you is the talent and gift gifted to you by God to make fruitful here on earth. If you do not make use of these talents, it will start suffocating you. You will have this feeling that you can do it, but other factors will come in your way. This storm within will roar within you.

I had the same storm within me making me uncomfortable each day, crippling my mind and soul. After along time I decided to scream so loud and let the inner beast within me be unleashed. Don't take this storm to your grave. Make use of what is given to you by God, not only to praise Him but also for your well being.

My friends I have seen people not believing in themselves and letting their talents die with them. That's the saddest part, letting life takeover you, instead of you taking control over your life. I would be more than happy to see everyone living their talents. If you can only imagine how the world would be where you would find each and every individual just living their dream, just doing what they love doing.

Now, though, it seems so far out of reach. I believe that it's not impossible. I have studied the lives of successful people who had just one vision and one belief and went with it, committed all the way till they reached the top. When you let the beast instinct within you come alive, the adrenaline takes you to the next level. Your sweat and blood and heartbeat keeps pumping to be best that you can be. Grow with success and deny all that stops you from being the undefeated beast. Because you are meant to win not once, not twice, but all the time. Don't tame the beast. Just let it ROAR.

Flying starts from the ground.
The more grounded you are,
the higher you fly.

- Anonymous

Chapter 51

Stay In Line

This is a very important chapter because I will discuss how not to go astray once you have achieved what you wanted. Success can be a blessing, but if you don't handle success properly it could lead to your destruction. Because once you go astray, you lose what you've worked so hard for.

The feeling of achieving what you always dreamed of cannot be compared with anything in the world. At the same time, the journey to that point also makes a person a better individual. Sometimes, the struggles in one's life ends up being a testimony to the world. While all the desires of the heart are given to you, don't give pride any room in your heart. Because pride has been the fall of many kingdoms in the past — let it not it be yours too.

I have seen a lot of people around me who have worked hard and have turned their efforts to success. They have reached the point where they had imagined themselves to be at. Being happy and proud is good, but when pride gets into your character and mind, how you handle it is very crucial. Success is always defined by character. Keep your attitude as humble as it was when you didn't have success. Let your success define you as an individual and a person who is down to earth.

Use your success story to benefit the masses. You may or may not be capable of making a change or being the change, but your words can always provide the spark to inspire crowds to make changes to their lives. The reason I chose 'Stay in Line' as the title of this chapter is because I wanted it to be a reminder to each and every one who reads this book. No matter how tall a plant grows, if its roots don't receive water, the plant stops growing and could eventually die. Always stay rooted to your base. Stay grounded. Stay in line.

The Finale

The road to success is not simple,
but the destination is where the
real joy lies.
- Sylvester Ryan Pontes

Chapter 52

Your Success Is My Success

My friends, there is nothing in this world that I world draw more pleasure from, than knowing that you benefited from this book. And that I was able to influence a change that would shape your life for the better. I have mentioned everything that I know that could help you.

I wrote this book so I could help someone who thinks they can't make it big if they come from a small background. This book is to encourage you and to tell you that I did it all from scratch. If you have the determination to live life on your terms and be successful, it is possible to do that.

The life of richness is not only for the rich. It is made for us too. And no one can rob your destiny from you. I read a quote from Grant Cardone that really ignited a spark within me to keep going non-stop. It encouraged me to up my effort 10 times and never settle for average. His quote said, "If you don't come from a rich family, make sure a rich family comes from you." I didn't come from an elite class, but I learned how to do it. With my experiences I hope you learn that your dream is possible to be achieved. Get it done at whatever price. We only live once. Don't just exist, but make sure you make a difference to others as well. My only prayer is that you end up living what your vision board states. And I would love to hear you success stories about your journey towards achieving them. The road to success is not simple, but the destination is where the real joy lies. I command you that with the power of the Almighty, go forth believing in your heart that you are an unstoppable force. And that you will never give up until you win. Because that is where I'd like to see each one of you. It doesn't matter if you're moving slowly, just make sure you're moving towards your goals.

Throughout your journey in life, don't
forget to have a good time.
                              - Sylvester Ryan Pontes

Chapter 53

Don't Forget To Have Fun

This is the last chapter of my book. I hope I have done justice in motivating you and in showing you that no matter who you are, where you are from, or what you are doing currently in your life, it is possible to achieve what you believe in. I also hope that this book is not simply motivation, but something that can inspire you to hear your soul and recognize your true calling.

This is an open confession about me; I was never a writer or an author. It really didn't fascinate me to read books when I was younger. I developed an interest in reading over time. Truly, the only reason I ended up writing this book was because I enjoyed the topic, and most importantly, it was fun. I would like to encourage your young minds to do what truly interests you and not something that gets you big money. Don't do something because the demand of that particular thing is higher in the market or because somebody else is doing extremely well at it. The sole purpose of me being a master of ceremonies and a speaker to inspire people was only because my interest lay in it and I loved doing it. Everything I have talked about are topics I enjoy personally. Had I not been enjoying it, I would have been a complete failure.

Hence, I encourage everyone to do something that makes you happy. Because if you're having fun, you will automatically get things done. I have seen many friends and even family, in jobs or careers they really don't enjoy. They travel to work every day, come back to bed, travel the next day with grumpy faces that hang to the ground kissing the dust. Don't let your situation be like them. When you go to work, you should spring out of your bed. Your face should be as radiant as the sun when you reach your workplace. The energy that you emit defines your true calling. Don't get into something that doesn't even make you want to wake up from your bed and leaves you unexcited. That is walking to self-destruction.

Do things that really bring a smile on your face because it's your smile, your interest, your talent, your inner self, and most importantly, your soul that matters. If all these things are rejoicing at what you are doing, then you're living the life of your true calling. It really wouldn't matter what amount of money you earn. Although money is important for living a life on earth, enjoying what you do is the real deal for life. I would love to witness everybody doing what they love doing, and live a five-day weekend life. It's not written in stone that one has to do a job to survive in this world. That's not what we've been called here for. We've been called to live a life of abundance. And that is only possible when we really understand what we are made for. When you start living your true calling every day, life ends up being a blessing.

As I end this chapter my only prayer is that the greatness which is bestowed within you is explored and shared with the whole world. May the light within you be used as a guide for others, to inspire them. And whatever you do in life don't you forget to have fun. May the blessings of the Almighty Father always be with you. May you have a splendid life in complete abundance. And may God be with you throughout your journey in life. Amen.

Biblical quotes I refer to when in need

Philippians 4:6 *"Do not be anxious about anything, but in everything, by prayer and petition, with thanksgiving, present your requests to God."*

Jeremiah 29:12 *"Then you will call on me and come and pray to me, and I will listen to you."*

Mark 11:24 *"Therefore I tell you, whatever you ask for in prayer, believe that you have received it, and it will be yours."*

Psalms 18:6 *"In my distress I called to the Lord; I cried to my God for help. From His temple He heard my voice; my cry came before Him, into His ears."*

Isiah 41:10 *"So do not fear, for I am with you; do not be dismayed, for I am your God. I will strengthen you and help you; I will uphold you with my righteous right hand."*

Inspirational Quotes by the Author

No one can rob your destiny from you.

Hustling is the real building of character.

Make yourself so valuable, that every word you utter becomes a quote.

Those who hustle end up living the life others dream of.

Let your tongue always be an instrument of praise and encouragement to others.

Don't pay heed to what others think, just do your thing.

Never prove your success to others. Let your work speak.

In the process of making money be conscious not to make the wrong move to attain it.

If you do something that will change or impact people's lives they will remember you till eternity.

Your work is a reflection of you. When you add your heart to it, then it's not only your work that radiates, it's your soul too.

Let not hatred be the reason for you to succeed.

Have the guts to break free from what you don't believe in.